The
Classic Guide

to
Winter Sports

The
Classic Guide
to
Winter Sports

ARNOLD LUNN

Editor of Climber's Club Journal and

Alpine Ski Club Annual

Illustrated
London
Eveleigh Nash
1913

AMBERLEY

Originally printed by: Ballantyne & Company, Ballantyne Press,
London
This edition first published 2015

Amberley Publishing
The Hill, Stroud, Gloucestershire, GL5 4EP
www.amberley-books.com

ISBN 978 1 4456 4890 3 (print)
ISBN 978 1 4456 4891 0 (ebook)

British Library Cataloguing in Publication Data.
A catalogue record for this book is available from the British
Library.

Typesetting by Amberley Publishing.
Printed in Great Britain.

Contents

Editor's Note

In the preface to the original version of this text, titled simply Skiing, Arnold Lunn commented that three texts on the subject were already available by the time of the 1913 publication of this handbook. To have just three detailed books on a sport as widely followed as skiing is today almost inconceivable; a notion which itself is thanks to early skiers such as Lunn, who persuaded people onto the slopes with the creation of guidebooks such as this one.

Skiing itself has a long history, stretching back almost five millennia; although this was often as a method of transportation as opposed the winter sport that we know and love today. While there is evidence that it may have been practised in what is now China in around 600 BC, modern skiing as we know it has its roots later on in Scandinavia. From around the mid-nineteenth century skiing experienced a boom in popularity, becoming a favourite sport and recreational activity for many. It was during this time that skiing began being undertaken professionally as a competitive sport; the first public ski competition was held in Norway in 1843.

Ski enthusiast and author, Arnold Lunn, was first introduced to the sport by his father. His enjoyment of skiing evidently stayed with him in his early years, as during his time studying at Oxford he founded the Oxford University Mountaineering Club. At the time of this guidebook's publication in 1913 Lunn was also the editor of Climber's Club Journal and Alpine Ski Club Annual. He later went on to establish several ski clubs, including The Alpine Ski Club (1908), Public Schools Alpine Sports Club (1919, and Kandahar Ski Club (1924). He also went on to organise many races around the world and has had a lasting impact on competitive skiing; it was thanks to his efforts that the slalom and downhill races were included for the first time in the Olympics in 1936. Lunn's enthusiasm and efforts for the professional practice of skiing were awarded in 1952 when he was knighted for his services to British skiing and Anglo-Swiss relations.

This book was originally intended to be a guidebook for beginners and in many ways it still serves that purpose well. Lunn started the text by covering the very basics of the sport, he provided details to the reader of where to purchase an outfit and how to select a sound ski instructor. He went on to give advice on how to perform turns, swings and jumps in the correct style; he recommended locations to ski and discussed the popular ski routes of the time; and outlined the origins of ski clubs. The guide was finished with a detailed and amusing recollection of Lunn's various ski trips and tours.

All in all, this classic guide continues to make a detailed introduction to winter sports for beginners, just as Lunn intended over 100 years ago; while at the same time it provides a wonderful insight into the world of skiing during a period when the delights of the sport were only just being discovered by many.

Becky Cousins (Editor)

Preface

Three books have already appeared in English on skiing, and each of them deserves careful attention. Rickmers writes primarily as a mountaineer; Richardson, the father of English skiing, has written perhaps the best comprehensive sketch of the sport, and his chapter on jumping is the best thing of its kind in any language; Caulfeild's analysis of the various swings and turns is considered by good Continental judges to be as valuable as anything that has yet appeared on the subject.

There should, however, be room for a cheap handbook to skiing, largely devoted to the needs of the beginner. During fourteen years I have visited practically every Alpine centre that has attracted ski-runners. I have tried to give the absolute novice some information on the choice of a centre and on the purchase of his outfit. The chapters on the technical side of skiing will, I hope, be sufficient for his

purposes. As he becomes more expert he will find Caulfeild's book
of great service since he devotes far more space than has been at my disposal to the various skiing movements. I hope, however, that nothing of importance has been omitted in my briefer sketch, for I have tried to touch on every aspect of skiing that is of interest.

There is another class of reader to whom I hope to appeal. Caulfeild began his book with a fiery introduction in which the British runner was taken to task for his lack of dash and style. As a result our complacency has been rudely shaken and there has been a marked improvement in British skiing.

Caulfeild, and Richardson for that matter, are concerned with the art of skiing, and neither of them is, strictly speaking, a mountaineer. Though they have filled the average runner with a conviction of sin, it still remains to raise the standard of British winter mountaineering. Here our standard is even lower than in other branches of skiing. Every year hundreds of Continental runners make guideless tours among the high Alps, but the average Englishman is quite content with mountains eight or nine thousand feet high, and if he reaches the summit of the Wildstrubel he fancies that he has reached the limit of safe skiing. The number of English runners who have done first-class work in the Alps might be counted on the fingers of both hands. One frequently hears a man explain a bad and nervous style by remarking that he is a winter mountaineer, and has no time for 'fancy tricks'. On inquiry this winter mountaineering usually resolves itself into ascents of the Bonderspitze or Schilthorn. The Alpine Ski Club has helped to make the high Alps better known to British runners, but our record is still deplorably low.

I have added a chapter of recollections in the hope that my experience may help to remove the exaggerated idea of the difficulty and danger which still clings to the winter Alps. Judged by Continental standards my climbs are very humble, commonplace achievements, and I hope that those who have the patience to read this book may be induced to leave the lesser hills and discover for themselves the joys of this the most fascinating of all forms of mountaineering.

No writer on skiing can wholly escape the charge of plagiarism. There is a certain fund of knowledge common to all ski-runners, and it is not easy to paraphrase the description of, say, a stemming turn, so that it shall read with all the freshness of novelty. In self-defence I may state that I was skiing before Caulfeild, Rickmers, and Professor Roget, but at the same time I gladly acknowledge my debt to them. Caulfeild especially has been of great service. He has read through my manuscript and helped me with many criticisms. Our occasional disagreements have been chiefly a matter of temperament. Caulfeild is a bold and first-class runner, and his experience is chiefly confined to slopes below the summer snowline. I am writing mainly for mountaineers, and certain unpleasant experiences above the snowline have filled me with a wholesome respect for the dangers of the craft. I never possessed the nerve to become a first-class runner, and a serious accident has condemned me for ever to the ranks of the second rate. So I trust that those who meet me on the skiing field will refrain from discovering the faults which I have condemned in my own inferior practice.

Now it only remains to express my sincere thanks for the valuable help I have received. Those who have tried to photograph turns and swings will appreciate the success which has attended Mr Fulton. He has kindly placed his splendid series at my disposal. He has also helped with much valuable information on Norway and Lapland, where he has done excellent pioneer work. His book *With Ski in Norway and Lapland* is invaluable to the ski-runner in those countries. Mr Rickmers, Dr Hoek, Mr Cadby, and Mr Richardson have come to the rescue with photographs, for which I am deeply grateful. Messrs. Rickmers and Roget have also permitted me to quote from their excellent books, which permission has kindly been confirmed by Mr Fisher Unwin, their publisher. To Caulfeild I have already expressed my gratitude. This generous assistance has been another proof of the freemasonry which exists among ski-runners.
Arnold Lunn

Introduction

Skiing versus Skating and Tobogganing | Where to Purchase an Outfit | How to Learn Skiing | Ski Teachers | A Graduated Course for the Novice | The Question of Style and the Problem of the Stick

Skiing versus Skating and Tobogganing

This book is written primarily for beginners. It is chiefly written for those who have never yet visited the winter Alps, and who are utterly ignorant of all matters of outfit and expenditure. To these I would say make up your mind that you would like to ski. Before you leave England you may perhaps fancy that you are going to skate or toboggan. You may believe that skiing is a vastly dangerous sport fitted to the young and adventurous. Possibly you may add that skating is possible in England, which seems to some a reason for neglecting everything else in the Alps. I have never been able to understand this position unless it is equivalent to saying that the skater has more opportunity of displaying his prowess in England than the ski-runner, and therefore that skating should be learnt in the Alps before skiing. I should, however, like to lay the following considerations before the reader. However anxious you may be to practise turns from dawn to sunset, the rink will not always be at your disposal. There will be days of thaw when the ice is closed, when even the most persistent of skaters must turn elsewhere for amusement. Those who toboggan will likewise find their runs impracticable, and curlers, skaters, and toboggan-riders will have to choose between bridge and skiing. This is where the ski-runner scores. His surface is not artificial. Wherever and whenever there is snow he can hope for sport, and in any centre worthy of the name he should be able to ski on practically every day through the winter. Even when long expeditions are impossible, he will be able to practise jumping, for the run out can be built up from time to time with fresh snow. As to tobogganing there are very few centres where this is considered as a serious sport. Twenty people ride the Creste from start to finish every year; elsewhere tobogganing is regarded as a means of transit from the hotel to the skating rink, or as a mild amusement for those too old to curl. Bobsleighing is another matter, but this again is the amusement of the minority. And so the novice to winter sports may fairly assume that he will sooner or later be forced into skiing. He will find the most unlikely folk starting forth on long tours, not only adventurous youths, but elderly men and even elderly ladies. Before he has been out a week he will be absorbed in fierce discussions on style and bindings and the correct method of marking jumps.

Where to Purchase an Outfit

In another chapter I have dealt at length with the whole question of outfit. Let me say, by way of preface, that the ordinary beginner has very little idea of setting about his purchases. He walks into a shop and announces that he is going to the Alps for Christmas and would like to be suitably fitted up. He is lucky if he emerges without a pair of curling stones, skates, a toy toboggan, and quite comic ski all wonderfully and fearfully made. Skiing boots and clothes can be bought in England as well as elsewhere, but ski are cheaper and better abroad. I always advise people to send an outline of their foot without stockings to Herr Björnstad, Bern, or any other good Swiss firm, such as Och Frères. They should enclose with this elegant sketch a note of their height. The boots and ski will then be sure to match, and may be sent care of the porter to the hotel in which their owners have booked rooms. They will be paid for on delivery by the porter, who should be advised beforehand by a post-card, and they will be found awaiting their owner on arrival. In a book of this description, intended more especially for novices, one may be pardoned for stating much that seems obvious to more advanced readers. And I will add to the foregoing the following summary. Make up your mind that you are going to ski and that you will probably take up skiing seriously. Boots must not be a matter of economy, and it is essential to buy them from a good firm. Ski can be borrowed at all Swiss centres, but such ski will be second-rate and will not fit as well as ski bought to order with your boots. I suggest that the beginner should read carefully the chapter on outfit and buy his clothes in England. He should then send a letter to some good Swiss firm, *i.e.* those that are allowed to advertise in skiing journals, couched in some such form as the following:

Dear Sir, I enclose a sketch of my foot without socks. Please send a pair of good skiing boots to: A. Jones, Esq., c/o The Concierge, Hôtel des Alpes, Schönthal. 'Contre remboursement'. Send also a pair of goats'-hair socks. The boots should be large enough to allow me to wear these socks and two other pairs of stockings. Please also send a pair of ski with Huitfeld bindings. I am anxious to secure a good grain. My height is 5 foot 10 inches. I also need a pair of stout sticks, a pair of waterproof gloves, and a woollen helmet.

I arrive at the Hôtel des Alpes on December 25, and I wish to find the ski waiting for me. I do not want to pay more than Fr.36 for the boots or Fr.35 for the ski.

It should be noted that ladies' boots will be somewhat cheaper. A line should also be sent to the concierge advising him of this order. It is unnecessary to enclose a cheque as the bill can be paid on arrival. The gloves will cost about 5s, the woollen helmet about 2s. The boots are more expensive and will probably cost about 28s. A very good pair of ski can be bought for 27s, and cheaper ones will stand a lot of knocking about. Sealskins can be bought later for about 10s. A complete outfit, including rucksack (from 6-12s), ski, boots, gloves, sticks, sealskin, and woollen helmet, will cost about £3 15s; these are the essentials. As the novice becomes more expert he will add a lantern, axe, and rope to his outfit; but, good boots, good ski, and good gloves he must have.

In another chapter I have dealt at length with the question of the best centres for skiing. And in an appendix I have quoted fares to the various centres.

How to Learn Skiing

One is often asked how long it takes to learn skiing. I should say that up to a point skiing is much easier to learn than skating. No one can hope to get much enjoyment out of skating until he has had at least a week's steady practice. Even then he will only be able to go straight forward and he may spend a good three weeks on the ice before he is able to cut a decent three. Now any able-bodied novice should be able to make an easy tour, involving, say, 2000 feet of ascent, after four hard days of practice. I have known a ski-runner cross the Wildstrubel on his third day, and have seen ladies put up a very good show on a long expedition after two days' practice. Such feats are rather exceptional, but the novice should be able to hold his own in an average party after a week's solid skiing. Much, of course, depends on the way he sets to work. If he puts himself under a good teacher and masters some good skiing book, he will save himself a lot of time and trouble.

So far, the comparison is all to the advantage of skiing. To become a moderately proficient ski-runner is easier than to attain the same standard in skating. To become a first-class runner is considerably harder than to become a first-class skater. I should be inclined to bet that of two men of equal capabilities the man who took to skating would have passed his first-class test some time before his friend had passed the first-class skiing test. To jump twenty-five metres is an athletic feat demanding great nerve and skill, far more nerve than is necessary for the most fearsome rocker, and just as much skill.

Another point often raised is the age of the beginner. Some folk seem to think that no one can become a first-class runner unless he has been born on ski. I think this is a mistake. And I imagine that a man who has once learned to jump correctly will go on jumping to an advanced age. Skiing is less a matter of brute force than of knack, nerve, and balance. As long as a man has strength enough to climb a hill, he will have strength enough to run down it providing he has already acquired the instinct for balance. No one could hope to become a first-class high jumper unless he had a certain combination of strength and spring denied to ordinary mortals, but any man with decent nerve and normal balance should be able to make long jumps if he gives the time to it. To make abnormally long jumps is another matter, but I should think that a jump of twenty-five metres is just within the powers of any man of normal strength who gives up the necessary time to the sport.

What constitutes a first-class runner? In the old days any man who made long tours on ski and did not often fall was considered a good runner by British critics. I look back with regret to the days when the standard was so easy of access. We have now become more critical, and even among British runners a man would not be considered an efficient performer unless he could run at a good speed without using the stick.

Skiing differs from many sports in that much can be learned from books. Very little can be learned of cricket from books, and even good coaches cannot do much with a pupil who has not a good foundation of instinctive skill. Skiing, on the other hand, is far less a matter of knack than some people suppose. The various turns and swings depend much more on the correct weighing of the ski, which may be learned from books or from good teachers. Let me give an example. My Telemarks had always been an uncertain quantity until I read Caulfeild's book. The moment I grasped two points I had no further difficulty. Caulfeild tells you to edge the front ski, take the weight off the back ski, and not attempt to force the turn. There is no knack needed to follow out these directions, and once they are grasped the Telemark is easy. Now you may tell a man to keep his eye on the ball, swing slowly back and follow through, and yet he may fail to drive a good ball, but I would guarantee to teach any beginner to do a Telemark at a slow speed after an hour's practice. A Telemark at a high speed can be learned by diligent perseverance, but even this alarming manoeuvre is far less a matter of knack than people suppose. And the same is true to a modified extent of jumping. Once realised, not only theoretically but subconsciously, that a fall will not hurt, that you are not launching yourself over a precipice, and you have only to make a decent 'sats' in order to clear a good distance. And the 'sats' itself can be largely learned from books. What you cannot learn except by experience is that jumping is a particularly safe, if superficially alarming, manoeuvre. I have not learned that yet.

Ski Teachers

Good teachers are not easy to find. A good teacher should be a good runner, but he need not be absolutely in the front rank. As long as he make all the turns and swings in correct style and at a fair pace, he is quite proficient enough to teach others. There is no difference of principle between a Telemark at twenty-five miles an hour and the same swing at forty miles an hour. He should be able to jump, but here again if he can jump fifteen metres in good style h can put the beginner on the right way just as surely as if he could jump thirty metres. It is far more important that he should perform all his turns, swings, and jumps in a perfect style than that he should do them at a very great speed or make very long jumps.

Besides being capable of skiing well, he must understand precisely why he skis well. That is where your good Norwegian is so often a failure as a teacher. He does his swings by inherited instinct. He has learned them as a child, and he is very genuinely puzzled when the beginner fails to imitate him. 'You just run downhill so,' I once heard a Norwegian remark to a beginner, as he darted down a slope of thirty degrees, 'then you swing your body round so and pull up with a Telemark'. The latter half of the instructions filtered through a cloud of snow thrown up as he swung round some twenty yards lower down. The Swiss guide is open to the same objections. To become a good teacher a certain type of educated mind is an advantage. I don't mean that an Oxford degree is any assistance to a ski teacher, but I think that a man who has been in the habit of analysing cause and effect in any branch of science will seize more readily on the cause of failure in his pupils than a teacher with no such training. The good teacher must be able to diagnose readily and accurately the various faults of his beginners, and must understand their difficulties. Where these are due to funking or laziness he should be in a position to point out the fact and give some salutary moral advice. The Swiss guide is not in such a position as long as he is in sight of a hotel. Above the snowline he is not unduly oppressed by the fictitious social values, but unfortunately the average ski course does not take place above the snowline. Lastly, the teacher should have complete command over his pupils' language, and for that matter over his own. A guide trying to explain the elements of a swing in broken English is not an inspiring sight.

There are at present two Englishmen who teach skiing professionally, and one could not wish for better mentors. There are also a number of amateur teachers. Some of these are good and keen, and if they teach the correct style they are giving valuable services to their fellow-men. But woe betide the beginner who puts himself under a keen but bad runner. He is almost sure to copy the bad qualities and avoid the good advice of his teacher.

A Graduated Course for the Novice

Besides good teaching something more is needed. And that, as Caulfeild has pointed out in an admirable article in the *Winter Sports Review*, is a good graduated course. The following course is partly adapted from that suggested by Caulfeild, and is partly the result of my own experience. I should advise the beginner to spend his first day in getting the feel of his ski. He should not be too eager to start downhill. I once heard a lady complain that the first time she put on ski she was expected to go downhill. There is a certain grain of sound sense in this whimsical complaint. The novice should spend his first half-hour walking on the level, kick turning, and getting into the position for straight running in normal and Telemark position. He should then select a slope of hard snow and walk up it, try a kick turn on a slope, herring-boning, and side-stepping. By this time he will have got the feel of the ski, and if he devotes a good hard hour of practice before trying to go downhill he will not feel so deplorably at sea when that alarming moment arrives. He may then begin to run downhill. A moderate slope of beaten snow is the best thing to practise on. It is not necessary to insist, as Caulfeild does, that he must practise getting up from a fall. There is plenty of practice in this branch of the art without going out of the way to invent opportunities. When he can run downhill in normal position without falling unduly often, he should find somewhere to run across the slope, and to run down it in Telemark position. This latter is excellent for the balance. I don't, as Caulfeild does, advise him to try anything further on the first day. If he can descend a slope of, say, twenty degrees without falling he has done as much as can be expected of him on the first attempt. On the second day, let him begin with a few straight runs and then get into stemming position on the level. When he has got hold of the position on the level let him then try it on a mild slope, varying his pace by first weighting the upper and then the lower ski. At the end of the second day he should have a very fair idea of stemming and be able to traverse a steep slope at a good angle by its help. He should also find some soft snow and practise the snow-plough position.

I hold very strongly that no beginner should try to do a downhill turn until he has been two full days, if not more, on ski. I know that I have Caulfeild against me on this point, and if Caulfeild can teach his pupils the Christiania the first day out, his powers of suasion must be well developed. Personally I think that if the beginner gets a good grasp of stemming, straight running in normal and Telemark position he will have done as much as can be expected of him in two days.

On the third day he should try a downhill stemming turn, and he should get his teacher to explain the movement on the level. The beaten-down practice ground is just the place to try this manoeuvre.

If he is very keen to try an expedition he may find some indulgent friend to take him a short run, say 1500 or 2000 feet. He will find practice-ground work a very different thing from skiing on tour. He will tumble about a great deal, and be puzzled at the apparent falling off in his running.

This need not alarm him. Better ski-runners come to grief when they are tired, and the beginner will be hopelessly tired. I advise him not to use sealskins for his first tours, as he had far better learn to climb a hill on naked ski. Let him, on this his first tour, try and make use of the stemming turn which came so easily on the practice ground. If, on his first tour, he does half a dozen downhill stemming turns without a stick, he has the makings of a good runner. He will, however, be well advised to put off this expedition until he has had four or five days of hard work on the practice ground, though perhaps a short 1000foot run might be attempted on his third day.

The third day's practice should be devoted to improving his straight running and his downhill stemming turn. He should also practise the jumping position on an ordinary slope. Let him run downhill and make his 'sats' at a given point, then drop into Telemark position. If he has time he can also try uphill Christianias from a traverse. The fourth day's practice should follow the same lines. Perhaps he may even try a small jump, but I advise him to get the 'sats' quite perfect before he goes over the smallest take off. He should improve the Christiania and try the Telemark. From this point there is no need for detailed instructions.

The Question of Style and the Problem of the Stick

Everything in skiing depends on a good start, and the beginner will do well to master the correct style in the early stages. We who began to ski in the early days, when the novice was taught to cling to his pole much as a drowning man clings to a straw, know well the labour of altering a style when once it has become a habit. So to the beginner I would say: Cultivate the narrow track and the free stickless running from the first day, and then, and then only, you may perhaps learn how to use a stick in the very few cases where a stick is necessary.

English skiing has gone through various stages, and I would refer the reader who is interested in the history of his sport to Chapter 9 of this book.

The early English ski-runners learned a villainous style. I remember my first lessons in 1898. We were armed with a vast staff, and taught to lower ourselves down slopes clinging to it with desperate zeal. Stemming turns and swings were entirely unknown. If we wanted to make a sudden change of direction we stopped and did a kick turn. If we wished to stop suddenly we sat down.

Then came Rickmers preaching the great gospel of Zdarsky, and for a time captured English skiing for the Austrian school. Lately a reaction has set in. Richardson and Caulfeild have taken us to task for timorous running, and the stickless style of Norway has become fashionable. I believe that this is the correct style and that the Lilienfeld system is a bad one; but, on the other hand, I think that Caulfeild, who goes a long way beyond Richardson in his attack on 'stick-riding', is something of a bigot. The point at issue is, roughly, this: Rickmers was primarily a mountaineer. His teaching embodies the sound teaching of the Alpine Club, the subordination of dash and display to sound, safe methods. He is primarily concerned with teaching the raw beginner to run with safety on difficult ground. He turned out in an astonishingly short space of time men who could be trusted to go on a long expedition without endangering the safety of the party and without keeping anybody back. With this in view, he relied entirely on the stemming turn with the stick, dismissed Telemarks and Christianias as graceful 'extras', and by no means discouraged people from using the stick.

Now let us see what Caulfeild has to say of this system. In his admirably direct preface to *How to Ski* he tells us that 'the main object of Zdarsky's system is to enable a runner-beginner to run safely on steep and difficult ground with the least possible preliminary practice ... it turns out ski-runners quickly by allowing them to run badly . . . the whole end of the system is to dispense with skill rather than with effort. . . next to caution, the most prominent characteristic of English running is bad style'.   There is much truth in these criticisms, but I think Caulfeild forgets that Rickmers is writing primarily for mountaineers, for whom ski are chiefly important as a means to an end. There is, of course, not the least reason why a man who climbs on ski should not run in the Norwegian style, but the average Englishman who spends, perhaps, three weeks abroad every winter and is anxious to devote as much of that as possible to long tours, resents the time wasted on the practice ground, and is quite happy if he can get through a tour with as few spills as possible. He comes, perhaps, to the sport late in life, when his nerve and dash are on the wane, and for him an intelligent use of the stick and a complete command of the stemming turn are possibly the essential things. And this, Rickmers teaches.

I believe, however, that a correct style is far easier to acquire than most people suppose, and that the most elderly runner could master all the turns and swings. He will naturally run with more caution than younger men, but even so he will be well advised to reduce stick-riding to a minimum and to master swings to right and left. To the beginner I would give this advice: Learn first of all without the stick, cultivate the narrow groove, master the stemming turn before learning the swings, and try to learn

How to Do It

How Not to Do It

the improved stemming turn, which has been nicknamed the 'stemmiania'. When you have thoroughly mastered the stemming turn and can make use of it on difficult steep snow, you should learn the Christiania swing to both left and right. It is far more generally useful than the Telemark.

You will now be able to go on any expedition as far as your skiing is concerned; the rest is a matter of physique. Your running will be very fair and far better than the average performances of the skiing Briton, provided that you do not use your stick and that where possible you run with your ski together. You are now ready to learn uphill Telemarks to a standstill and downhill linked Telemarks. Neither of these swings is a necessity, but the downhill Telemark is a much more graceful turn than the stemming turn. It is also possible to do it at a higher speed, and in soft snow it requires far less effort. But remember that the stemming turn is the key to all difficult running, and no man is really fit to carry out big tours unless he has complete control of it.

From the very first day that you put on ski carry two sticks. A pair of sticks is much more useful than a single stick uphill and on the level. Downhill they have this advantage. If you are using a single pole, it is a great temptation to slip both hands on it and lean on it on difficult ground. If, on the other hand, you have a pair of sticks, you must put them together if you intend to use them as a brake. This calls for a much more conscious effort, and inspires the offending runner with a much more definite conviction of sin than a surreptitious grip of the single pole. Remember that beyond a certain point improvement is impossible without conscious effort. I know this to my cost. I had become a fairly steady runner ten years ago, and was accustomed to make long tours regularly throughout the season. I did not fall much, and I could turn pretty readily on most ground by judicious use of my stick. But I never made any progress. There was a certain speed, a very low speed, at which I was fairly comfortable, and I never tried to go beyond this speed. Nor did I make any attempt to learn swings of which I knew nothing. I became steadier each season, but I did not improve in skill or dash.

And this is a very typical case. One becomes so enthusiastic about climbing that one cannot bear to sacrifice a day on the practice slopes. If you wish to go on improving you must put in hard practice days between expeditions. On a tour you are too tired to make experiments. You want to get back for dinner, and if you start falling you feel that you are keeping the party back. So I advise you to give up one day a week, this is the bare minimum, to hard practice, and don't be content with doing your swings on the practice ground. Try them the next day on tour. So many people can do their swings and turns on the slopes near the hotel and break down hopelessly on a mountain.

Above everything, don't allow yourself to fall into a groove. Make a deliberate mental resolution at the beginning of each run to raise the limit of speed at which you can run with comfort. Pull yourself up sharply when you feel that you are not trying to make progress. Don't get into the way of relying on a particular turn or swing for all emergencies. Practise all the turns and swings, and use the turn that is adapted to the snow, not the turn in which you are most proficient. Moreover, don't deceive yourself into imagining that you are practising turns when you are really only shirking the straight run. Turns and swings are not, as in skating, an end in themselves. The best ski-runner is the man who can traverse difficult ground at the highest speed without falls. Swings and turns are only an unavoidable alternative to straight running.

Try and get to know the local runners. There is nothing better for you, if you are beginning to fancy yourself as a runner, than a day's tour with the local club.

Some criticisms of Caulfeild. The advice given in the preceding paragraphs is the same in tendency as the gospel which Caulfeild preaches with such vigour. It is simply the essence of the Norwegian style, but at the same time Caulfeild is, in my humble opinion, somewhat fanatical in his views of stick-riding. After all, skiing is radically different from skating in this respect. In skating there are certain turns which constitute the whole duty of the figure-skater. They are literally an end in themselves. A man does not do a forward rocker because his pace is too high and he is in some danger of colliding with the bank. And the manner in which these turns must be done is a matter of rigid and artificial interpretation. Their whole object being to look graceful, any movement which is anaesthetic must be avoided.

There are those (although Caulfeild is not one of them) who would treat skiing turns and swings from the same standpoint, and would regulate the precise way in which a Christiania must be carried through by a code as strict as that which governs the position of the unemployed foot in English skating. But the saner view regards swings and turns as a means to an end, and not as a spectacular tour de force.

There is no objective definition of style. The narrow groove, the stickless turn, are only good style in so far as they help a man to run more safely, more swiftly, and with less effort. The moment that the stick saves effort without diminishing the speed there seems no prima facie reason why it should not be used. Some of the best Norwegian runners ski with knees bent and feet apart and almost level. They ignore the Telemark turn and only rarely use the Christiania, and their method of turning downhill is to slow up by snow-ploughing and step round. But when they came over to the Continental meetings they carried all before them (*Winter Sports Review, April 1912*). My guide, Maurice Crettex, with whom I skied for a month last season, had no notion of how to Telemark or Christiania, and I remember a young lady's remark to the effect that he was a stick-rider. She said this as if it completely disposed of his claims to be considered a good runner. To which I replied that he had beaten all the guides in his district in the local race, that he thought nothing of taking slopes of forty degrees straight and that he never fell, that he invariably arrived at the bottom before the rest of the party concealed in a cloud of snow thrown up by his stick, and that he was the fastest runner I had met. Re: stick-riding, Captain Dahl, the President of the Norwegian Ski Association, says: 'Concerning the general use of the stick in cross-country running downhill, it may be said that it is of great help for swinging, regaining the balance, and diminishing the pace. In many cases it is even necessary. It is better to do without it as long as possible, but when you feel no longer safe, the use of the stick is perfectly legitimate'.— *Winter Sports Review*.

The question seems to be: Which is the better runner—a man who gets there first with an ugly style or a man who has a good style but comes in second?

I raised this point with Caulfeild, and he remarked that Rickmers might have had a better case had he stated frankly that he taught the bold use of the stick instead of quibbling with such phrases as 'an occasional dab at the slope'. Certainly we of the older school did learn to use our sticks on rough country in a way which was undoubtedly useful. Crettex is a good example of this method, and I would

Straight Running

back Crettex against most Norwegians in a
mere matter of pace plus steadiness. Caulfeild
states dogmatically that, with the possible
exception of narrow icy paths the stick is never
of any use. I do not deny that on any ground
on which a stick-rider could turn a stickless
runner could also turn, but I assert without

any fear of contradiction in ambulando that on steep, hard snow the man who boldly turns on his stick as a pivot will make a sharper, neater turn than the stickless runner, for the simple reason that the latter is bound to skid further, as the stick tends to check the slide down the slope. To deny this is to deny those principles of physical law which Caulfeild has applied so skilfully in his analysis of the various swings. Richardson, Delap, and others with whom I have discussed this point agree that there are occasions on which a bold use of the stick is a material assistance. My point is simply this. There is nothing indecent about a stick, and if its use enables you to make a sharper turn on hard snow than would otherwise be possible a stick turn is good style, especially where skidding (which is often useful to help out a swing) would be dangerous on account of some obstruction that necessitates a sharp turn.

So too with the narrow groove. The narrow groove is not good style because it looks pretty. It is good because in most conditions of the snow longitudinal stability is more valuable than lateral stability, and also because latitudinal stability is often actually secured by the narrow groove; *cf.* Caulfeild's ingenious analogy from bicycles versus tricycles. But the moment that latitudinal stability is seriously threatened, the narrow groove is no longer a paying compromise. I made experiments with a very good runner on hard wind-swept snow, and we both agreed that the narrow groove is a bad position on such snow, and that the steadiest method of descending was to keep the feet well apart. So that, according to my definition of style as that method of running which ensures steadiness and the maximum speed, the narrow groove would be bad style on hard snow, just as the broad groove is bad style on soft snow.

With these trifling qualifications, I agree with Caulfeild's attack on the use of the stick.

1

Outfit

The Ski: Wood and Grain | *Various Bindings* | *The Stick* | *Boots* | *Crampons* | *Clothing* | *Rucksack* | *Repair Outfit* | *Sealskins* | *Food, &c.*

The question of outfit is of vital importance, for faulty kit may mean frost-bitten extremities, and a bad binding will often result in broken bones. The whole question of outfit is still in the committee stage, but on certain essential points most experts agree. *The Alpine Ski Club Annual*, No. 3, contained a report based on a series of questions addressed to the club which every winter mountaineer should get hold of. The first point to consider is the question of the ski themselves.

The Ski: Wood and Grain

Ski are usually made of ash or hickory, but very serviceable ski can be manufactured from birch or pine. The lightness and cheapness of the latter woods are advantages, and they are suited to the needs of postmen and shepherds in snowy districts who might not, perhaps, be able to afford more expensive ski. They are not adapted to work involving big strains on the wood, such as jumping and mountaineering. Hickory is an excellent material. It is heavier than ash, but also more durable. The running surface is less liable to be badly scraped, but most runners seem to prefer good ash. Good ash is, however, becoming scarce, and you are less liable to get bad hickory than bad ash.

The grain: The best wood for ski is that cut near the bark, and the best ski are those with a wide grain, a natural deduction from the first statement which anybody can verify by examining the section of a tree as shown on the stump. The grain should taper up to the point, and should not run out at the sides. Grain which complies with these conditions is exceptional. Most grain runs out to some extent. If it runs out, it should do so in a direction from toe to heel. If it runs in the opposite direction, splinters will form and retard progress. Such ski are best broken up and put in the plate along with bad Fr.5 priced pieces.

To summarise: Avoid a close grain, a grain that runs from heel to too, or a grain that runs out under the foot or at the front bend. Needless to say, the ski should be as free as possible from knots.

There is one other point to be noticed in connection with the grain. If you examine the broad end of the ski you will find the grain disposed in one of the arrangements illustrated below.

Of these, A is bad, B a fairly good grain, and C thoroughly good.

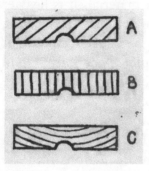

Diagram 1

The colour of the ski is a matter of individual taste. I have seen red ski which looked pretty when new, and black ski are very effective. Paint, however, is sometimes applied to conceal defects of grain, and coloured ski should be regarded with suspicion.

The height of the ski is an important point. Rickmers advocates short ski for mountaineering, and the average holiday-maker who does not make his turns with any certainty should avoid long ski. The skilful runner will not find extra length makes much difference to ease of turning, and for him long ski spell steady balance, smoothness over rough ground, and a straight course. A man of the usual proportions (some people have very short arms, and for them this test is useless) will select a ski whose tip he can just reach with the roots of his fingers when the arm is held straight out above the head. This is a good-sized ski, but it may well be somewhat longer. A short ski is one which he can touch with his wrist, applying the same test. For mountaineering over rough country a short ski has advantages, but if it is too short it develops irritating habits. A short ski wobbles while straight running and crosses behind when Telemarking. If you do a great deal of glacier running a long ski will, perhaps, prove safer. It distributes the weight more evenly and it runs at a greater speed, both important points in view of the danger caused by insecurely bridged crevasses. One occasionally meets people with stiff joints who find kick turns very tiresome. They will, of course, adopt short ski, unless they prefer Caulfeild's ironic advice to jump round instead of kick turning.

The ski should be narrow. It is a delusion common among beginners that broad ski are steadier. The first steep slope of hard wind-swept snow should cure them of this error. A man about 5 feet 10 inches in height should choose ski whose length is 85 inches and whose breadth at the binding should be less than 3 inches.

Ski are sold with and without a groove. The groove is a great assistance in straight running and its presence will not interfere with ease of turning save in the case of poor runners. An important point is the arch of the ski. This should be gradual and should be not more than f in. high at the highest point. The thickness of the ski will vary with the work for which it is intended. Mountaineers and jumpers will choose ski with a good thickness below the binding, though this concession to safety will mean a slight loss in comfort.

In order to strengthen a ski in relation to its weight, the ski is sometimes made with a convex upper surface. Strength is sacrificed to flexibility, and the total loss and gain about balance.

Various Bindings

Here we touch on highly controversial ground, and the beginner who is amused by the ferocity with which such questions are debated should read the story of the so-called battle of the bindings which I have told in Chapter 9. Briefly, bindings may be divided into sole bindings and heel bindings. A sound binding for touring should possess the following qualifications: (1) Strength. (2) Lightness as far as is consistent with strength. (3) It should be easily put on and off. In climbing one often meets short stretches best taken on foot. The man who can slip his ski on or off without trouble scores a great advantage. (4) It should admit of being easily repaired, and should be such that a duplicate binding can be easily carried and adjusted. (5) It should be capable of adjustment with gloves on. (6) It should be firm and yet give way under a violent strain. (7) It should permit a limited vertical and a still more limited lateral play, but in case of emergency the lateral play should be capable of yielding to a bad wrench.

Most bindings are a compromise. The binding that fulfils all the above qualifications has yet to be invented. There are numberless inventions on the market, but we propose to confine our attention to the leading designs which have divided the allegiance of most ski-runners.

Toe bindings. The Huitfeld binding with Ellefsen clamp is by far the most popular binding in Norway and on the Continent. It answers fairly-satisfactorily to the above requirements (1), (2), (4), (6). A handy duplicate Huitfeld binding is supplied by good firms, and this is a strong point in its favour for serious mountaineering. The safety of the binding is also a good asset, as if properly adjusted it will allow the foot a great deal of lateral play in the case of a bad fall. But to my mind it hardly deserves its great popularity. Unless the toe irons are fitted with the greatest accuracy, the boot refuses to remain in the middle of the ski. The straps soon wear out at the toe irons, and the heel strap checks the speed by brushing against the snow. Moreover, despite the clamp, it is not very easy to put on in a hurry, and the wider the radius of extension allowed by the clamp, the more effort is required to shut the clamp. The straps vary in tension with the temperature and work loose very easily, and though the lateral play is an advantage in the case of a bad fall, it makes steering less certain than with other bindings. Still it is undoubtedly a sound binding, and the beginner will not go far wrong with it if he adjusts it with care. He should see that his knee can just touch the ski when kneeling down, but he should not be able to kneel without some effort. Beginners sometimes thrust their r toes too far into the toe irons and then feel a grievance if they get a nasty wrench after taking a toss.

The Ellefsen is a favourite binding. It has the following advantages: The toes need not be thrust so far into the toe irons, as the lateral strain is divided between the toe irons and the heel pieces. Steering is easier than with the Huitfeld and the binding is easier to adjust, more especially if the back strap is fitted with an Ellefsen clamp. Its disadvantages are that it is not quite so safe as the Huitfeld and that it is difficult to repair if it breaks. Moreover, breakages are liable to happen. The binding has a way of wearing badly in certain places. The belting wears out under the toes, and the heel pieces often break off. The mountaineer who intends to go far afield, far away from the chance of getting a binding repaired, will run risks if he uses the Ellefsen, but for ordinary day tours it is far better than the Huitfeld. It must be added that as long as the toe irons do not give way it should be possible to adjust a Huitfeld spare binding, which should therefore always be carried.

The Black Forest binding. This used to be a very popular binding at one time, but has now gone out of fashion. It made steering very easy, but its extreme lateral rigidity was dangerous in the case of a fall. It was very strong and light, and breakages never occurred without long warning in the shape of fraying leather. It should be used with the Huitfeld toe irons, and the dummy heel and balata sole should be riveted together with aluminium. A strong advocate of this binding claimed in the *Alpine Ski Club Annual* that if it were properly fitted the snow would not ball between the heel and the binding. None the less, 1 do not think that it is in the same class as the other bindings mentioned.

Sole bindings. The Lilienfeld, Austria, and Bilgeri bindings are examples of sole bindings. As the Bilgeri is by far the best of the three, we will consider it first.

In a toe binding the point on which you turn when you kneel on the ski is somewhere near the ball of the foot. In sole bindings you turn in front of the toes. The foot is attached to a metal plate which is fixed to the ski in front of the toes by an ingenious hinge; a clever spring arrangement gives a degree of vertical rigidity which may be more or less controlled by a screw.

I always had a great dislike for sole bindings, but after breaking my leg I found that my toes were nearly rigid and that a fall forward in Huitfeld bindings gave me an agonising wrench, I could find no binding in which I could kneel on the ski, and after experimenting for a season with adaptations of the Huitfeld I reverted to the Bilgeri. There are many people who have stiff toes, and for them a sole binding is essential. I soon got to like the Bilgeri, and am not sure that it is not as good a binding as is on the market. It gives a great control for steering; it is much more easily put on and off than the Huitfeld or Ellefsen. It is claimed that lateral control is secured at the expense of safety, but I fancy that the shaped metal plate and the ordinary give in a boot will allow quite enough play for a bad fall. The lack of vertical control is certainly a nuisance. The binding is also impossible to repair on a mountain-side, and, like all other sole bindings, should never be used for jumping. The Lilienfeld and Austria bindings are inferior bindings on the same system.

Whatever binding is adopted, the part of the ski just under the foot should be covered with a thin plate of metal, such as brass or tin. This prevents the snow balling under the foot. With the Bilgeri and other sole bindings a plate of celluloid is sufficient.

The Stick

I strongly advise most people to carry two sticks. For reasons given in the Introduction they will then be far less tempted to stick ride. In rare emergencies, when a little stick riding may be necessary, these can be put together. Do not get the sticks which can be readily fastened together and made into a single pole. They are rather too prominent an advertisement of bad style. Two sticks are a great advantage uphill. Only buy those sticks which have a metal disk attached to the end. This makes a great difference in climbing, and if you are in the habit of helping out a Telemark with a prod of the stick, a diskless stick will sink in too far and probably upset you. The type of disk which is affixed by a thong passing through the stick is bad. A very convenient type is a disk which can be screwed on to any stick.

It is a mistake to get too light sticks, as they sometimes break when you lean on them on extricating yourself after a bad fall. (They have been known to break on other occasions, but that is another story.)

Boots

The boots are the most important part of the ski-runner's clothing. Cold hands can be rubbed in the snow or tucked away in a warm pocket, but cold feet are much less accessible. The boots should be large enough to admit a pair of socks, a pair of stockings, and a thick pair of goats'-hair socks, and for mountaineering yet another pair of socks of silk or paper are almost indispensable. I have come within an ace of frostbite with a pair of thick socks, a pair of goats'- hair socks and stockings, a thickness of paper and puttees, though my circulation is ordinarily extremely good. It is, however, no use padding a boot with socks or stockings unless your toes have plenty of room to move.

Get the best skiing boots, as supplied by Bjornstad, of Bern, or any other good firm. Skiing boots with a single seam down the middle are far and away the best. The old Laupaar pattern is best avoided. The boots are apt to wear away against the toe irons, and a good device is to screw thin plates of metal to the side of the sole at these points. The boots should be frequently greased and oiled. For mountaineering a felt toe cap is very convenient. I have bought these in Christiania and they can be taken on and off at will, but perhaps it is better to have them fixed once and for all.

Crampons

Ski-runners disagree as to whether boots should be nailed or crampons carried. It is a good plan to have a few light nails round the soles of the boots, but crampons are indispensable for long tours. Boots heavily nailed are apt to be cold, and nails do not work well on skiing boots. On the iced rocks that one gets in winter crampons are essential to safety. For most ordinary work the four-pointed crampons are sufficient, but if much ice and step cutting is anticipated eight-pointed crampons should be taken. The disadvantage of the latter is that they have to be tied on so tightly that they are apt to restrict the circulation.

Clothing

The important thing is to have some wind-proof rough material outside that does not collect snow. No experienced runner would dream of wearing a sweater outside, as the wind whistles through it like a knife and it collects all the loose snow. Burberry and Jaeger cloth are as good materials as any. A silk jacket as supplied by Bjornstad is very light, and almost wind and water-proof; it tears, however, rather easily. A paper waistcoat, as supplied by Bjornstad and other good firms, is very warm, lasts a long time, and is light and compact.

It is essential to have some kind of covering for the head which will, if necessary, protect the ears and chin. The ordinary *passe-montagne* is as good as most things. A silk tube is a very useful addition to one's kit. Always carry at least one silk scarf, which can be put on underneath the *passe-montagne* in really cold weather, as the latter lets the wind through.

Never go out without a pair of smoked spectacles, for though the sun is not so strong in winter as in summer, it is often quite bad enough to bring on a partial snow-blindness if the eyes are not protected.

Rucksack

The rucksack should be large, so that when the contents are packed it will lie flat against the back. A small wicker-basket arrangement between the back and the rucksack is very pleasant and keeps one's back cool. A rucksack at present sold in Stockholm distributes the weight better than any other rucksack on the market.

Repair outfit

One person in the party should carry a spare ski-tip. Mr Pery has invented a ski-tip which is better than those on the market. Clamps with screws should also be taken in case the ski breaks lower down. A spare binding is also essential if it is of the type that can be fitted on easily. For long mountain expeditions it may be worthwhile to take an extra emergency ski three feet long.

It is astonishing how very few ski-runners bother to take any bandages, &c., but it is almost criminal to start on a long expedition without some surgical or medical appliances, as a badly broken leg stands ten times as much chance of recovering if the wound is treated with antiseptic lotion and gauze immediately after the break. Burroughs and Wellcome have designed an admirable light, compact case containing everything that the ski-runner is likely to require in an emergency. The case, which costs half a crown, may be obtained from any chemist.

I would also suggest a few grains of morphia. One-eighth of a grain might be given safely in the case of an accident, and would make an enormous difference to the patient's comfort. I have often suffered from a headache after the first big climb of the season, followed by stiffness. This summer I experimented with sodium salicylate. The effects were magical. I lunched one day in London and slept next night at the Bergli, and thence crossed the Mönch. I felt perfectly fit throughout the climb, and experienced no stiffness on the following day. A tablet should be taken three times a day two or three hours away from food. Anybody with a tendency to gout will find this a valuable suggestion.

Some kind of knife should always be carried, and the sheath knife sold in Norway and Switzerland is very useful for scraping snow off and other odd jobs.

Sealskins

These are essential for all long tours, as they save at least 20 per cent, in time and labour. They should fit well and should be adjusted by clamps, not by a buckle. There is a variety on the market, the Sohm Madlener, which is adjustable by adhesive wax in the place of webbing or straps, but one hears such varying reports of this invention that I do not like to recommend it until I have seen it at work.

Ski-wax is sold either in tubes or in short hard bars. Ski-wax should always be carried, as it makes running much easier when the snow is inclined to slip.

Lantern. On all tours carry a lantern, as there is always a chance of having to do a great deal of skiing in the dark, if anything goes wrong. The ordinary folding lantern supplied for mountaineers should be used.

Food

This will be a matter of individual taste. I strongly recommend dried milk powder; it is light, more compact, and very nutritious. On a long tour some kind of luxury is almost a necessity, as one tires so of the ordinary commissariat. A pound of caramels makes a very welcome addition to one's provisions. Iced tea or coffee is the best drink. Grape Nuts should also prove useful.

I don't recommend climbing irons for ski, as if the snow is so hard as to necessitate their use one had far better take off one's ski and carry them.

Be sure to put some carrying straps in your rucksack. Short stretches of steep hard snow are best taken on foot. The two hands should be left free and the ski carried slung round the shoulders. It is not difficult to drop and lose an unstrapped ski.

Ice-axes are a great nuisance when skiing, and on ordinary mountain expeditions it is only necessary that the leader of the expedition should carry one. Some ski-runners carry a long ice-axe fitted with a disk and use it as a stick, but it is better to carry a short ice-axe and sling it over your back when not in use.

Mr Noelting, in the second number of the *Alpine Ski Club Annual* advocates that ski-runners, when crossing dangerous ground, should tie a coloured rope about sixty feet long round their waist and trail it behind them. This will give some clue to their whereabouts if they are buried in an avalanche.

Ropes carried in winter should be new and as strong as possible, as they are liable to very severe strains and break more easily in winter than in summer. Guides should not be allowed to use up their old summer ropes in winter, as this habit has resulted in more than one bad accident.

Firewood is now almost invariably to be found in club-houses, but inquiries should be made beforehand, and if there is no wood in the hut firewood must be carried up.

2

How to Ski

On the Level | Kick Turn | Uphill | Herring-Boning | Side-Stepping | Straight Running | Snow-Ploughing| Side-Slipping | Stemming | Telemark Swing | Christiania Swing | Jumping

The beginner should read Chapter I and note what is said there about style. He should make up his mind to learn each movement in the best style from the beginning, and he should master the two positions of straight running, the turns and the swings, on very gradual slopes before experimenting on steeper ground. It is not a bad plan to try the positions of a new turn or swing on the level before attempting them on a slope. Make a point every day of improving the speed of your running and, above all, try to avoid backward falls, as these are nearly always a sign of funking. In Norway the backward fall is considered a disgraceful thing, while a fall forward is considered a venial offence, as it is the result of exaggerating a daring position.

On the Level

The first step is to put on your ski, taking care that your toes do not protrude too far through the toe iron, or in the event of a severe fall you will get a bad wrench. They should protrude so far as to allow you just to kneel on your ski. On the level do not lift, but slide your ski, and keep them parallel and as near together as possible. Give a good lunge forward on the right foot, striking off with the stick in your left hand. Lean well forward with your stick as far back as possible after throwing your weight on to the leading foot. Don't bring the other foot up to it until the slide is nearly finished. You will go faster if you use two sticks. Four or five miles is a very fair pace on hard snow.

Kick Turn

The kick turn is an easy and indispensable manoeuvre. On the level. Lift the left ski with a sharp swinging movement, keeping the knee unbent and the front part of the ski well forward. You will thus assume the first position as shown in the illustration. Without stopping, swing the ski round outwards and downwards and lay it down beside the right

Kick Turn

ski as shown in the illustration. Then bring the right ski round parallel to the left ski. It is easy to do this without sticks, and in no case should you lean heavily on the sticks during the turn.

How to Ski On a slope

Where the slope is not too steep you had better start with the top foot. You should point the ski slightly uphill before beginning the turn. On a steep hill-side in deep snow it is perhaps better to begin with the bottom ski, and in this case remember to point the ski downhill before beginning the turn.

Uphill

If the gradient is not very steep, you may slide uphill in much the same manner as you slide forward on the level. As the hill steepens you will gradually reach a point where the ski begin to slip backwards. You can, however, advance at a steeper gradient than would at first appear possible. Don't try to slide your ski forwards, but raise their points a few inches and bring the ski firmly down with a gentle stamp. Lean back slightly and hold your body as nearly at right angles to the slope as possible. If you lean forward, your ski will slip away from you. You should feel that the pressure of the toe-straps is more obvious than on the level. The secret of climbing is to advance with a slight but firm stamping movement at each step. The ski must be laid down parallel to each other and at right angles to the slope. If you drag them backwards or thrust them forwards the ski are bound to slip. Confidence is the most important factor in success. Once you have got the feel of the thing and cease to believe that your ski are slipping, the rest is easy. Don't, however, try a steeper gradient than you can comfortably manage. Beginners waste valuable time by taking a hill steeper than their ski will allow.

Obviously, if you do not climb a hill straight you will sooner or later have to turn round and reverse your direction. Strike a line that will involve as few kick turns as possible, for they waste valuable time. While climbing, keep a stick in each hand. To put both sticks together is only advisable on the steepest slopes of hard snow. When, however, they are used together, they should be held towards the hill. Never alter the gradient at which you are climbing in order to take a short cut across a gully by running down into it and climbing the opposite side. Experienced ski-runners rarely change the gradient of ascent, and an apparently long detour at a uniform angle is always shorter than a descent followed by a steep if short climb.

Herring-Boning

Short steep bits may be tackled by a method known as herring-boning. Face the hill and plant the ski outwards, roughly, at right angles to each other. Climb the slope straight up, lifting the ski forward and placing them on their inner edges. The angle between the ski should remain the same throughout. On a steep slope this method is extremely fatiguing, but it is tolerably easy on a short stretch of ground which is just too steep to take straight.

Side-Stepping

Hold your ski horizontal and lift the top ski sideways uphill placing it again in a horizontal position. Bring the lower ski up beside it. Side-stepping is apt to be extremely slow, and a useful modification, known as half side-stepping, is to lift the upper ski forwards as well as sideways.

Straight Running

The beginner should practise this and all subsequent movements with a stick held in each hand, or with no sticks. If he uses a single stick he will very probably lean on it and employ it as a prop. If he once gets into the habit of using a stick, he will never become a first-rate ski-runner. Pluck is the most important element in straight running. Nine out of ten backward falls are simply due to funking pure and simple. The beginner will, therefore, do well to lean well forward. When he becomes more expert and no longer falls out of nervousness he will very rarely have an unexpected backward fall, and his balance is then far more likely to be upset by a sudden change from fast snow into sticky snow, which will throw him on his face. So that the advice 'Lean forwards', though excellent for the beginner, whose falls are nearly all backward falls due to pure nervousness, is subject to modification for the expert, who is far more likely to pitch forwards. The expert should guard against forward falls by keeping his front leg stiff and leaning slightly backwards, so as to check this tendency to pitch forward on reaching sticky snow. He need have little fear of falling backwards when once he has ceased to feel nervous at a high speed.

The beginner may draw comfort from the fact that, owing to air pressure, his pace will not increase after the first few seconds. It is while he is actually gathering way that the balance is most difficult. Forty miles an hour is about as fast as any one is likely to go except on very steep hills and after a big jump.

Starting a run. If you are at the top of a hill, you just take a few forward steps and slide over the edge. To start a run on steep ground is not so simple. A favourite but clumsy method is to prop yourself up with two sticks, point your ski downhill, shove off with your sticks, and start running. A much neater method, for which I think Caulfeild is responsible, is the following. Move the ski round so that they point as far downhill as possible without actually slipping. Then, if the hill is on your right-hand side, throw your weight on to your left ski, lifting round the right ski until it faces straight downhill, its tip being just in front of and below the tip of the other ski. Now throw all your weight on the right foot and lean well forward downhill. The right ski will begin to slide, and the left ski, if left to itself, will fall into its natural position for straight running.

Straight running, normal position. Hold the ski together and advance one foot about twelve to eighteen inches in front of the other. Straighten the front knee and throw nearly all the weight on to the back foot. Hold your knees together, keeping the body as erect as possible, and try to hold yourself loosely and avoid stiffness, more especially at the knees. It is not a bad plan to stiffen the front knee if there is any chance of running from fast into sticky snow. The reason of this is explained above.

It is important to keep the ski together. For a very clever argument in favour of the single track, I refer the reader to Caulfeild's clever analogy drawn from a comparison between a bicycle and a tricycle. The beginner may take it as proved that in ordinary good snow the single-track position is the best. A very good plan is to practise running down slopes trying to keep a handkerchief between the knees. I believe this device was invented by Zdarsky.

If the reader will turn to the paragraphs on jumping he will see that the jumper straightens out on leaving the jump, thus increasing the length of his jump. The average runner who wishes to stick to the snow instead of jumping will follow exactly the opposite procedure; he will crouch down on crossing a mound, bending the knees and letting the body sink, and will straighten up on crossing a dip. Roughly speaking, his body should be at right angles to the slope; therefore the steeper the slope the more necessary it is to tilt the body forward.

The single-track position is the best in good snow, but on hard snow it is necessary to keep the feet level and hold the ski a few inches apart. On such snow both knees should be bent considerably more than for normal running and the body should be tilted rather more forward. In running across a hill-side it is best to lead with the upper foot unless you are in the Telemark position, in which case you should lead with the lower foot.

On very steep hills and on alighting from a jump you should run in the Telemark position. You are far less likely to be upset by small obstacles, which are almost certain to cause your ski to leave the ground if you are running in the normal position. Slide the back ski backwards until its tip is about level with the ankle of the other leg. Throw all the weight on the front foot and bend the knee of the front leg almost to a right angle. The front leg from the knee downwards should be, roughly, at right angles to the snow. On bumpy ground the knee of the back leg will very often touch the ski. It is important to hold the single-track position throughout.

If you are using a sole binding you will find that the back knee is thrown on to the ski and that there is a tendency to kneel on the back ski. Sometimes the kneeling leg gets dragged off the ski into the snow, and if you are going at any speed a very nasty jar is the result. It has struck me that if a small hollowed leather pad were placed on the back ski so as to receive the knee, there would be less chance of this tendency for it to slip off into the snow, which is especially troublesome in the manoeuvre known as the Telemark stem. Caulfeild and I are going to experiment with some such 'Telemark' pad next winter, but until it has actually been tried it would be unsafe to recommend it. The well-known Norwegian runner, T. Björnstad, who has taken over Dethleffsen's business in Bern, has written to me a letter in which he expresses himself very strongly against the Telemark position and the Telemark stem.

An alternative to the Telemark position, which is rather less tiring to hold, is the crouching position. Hold the ski in much the same position as for the normal running position and crouch low down, almost sitting on the back heel.

When you fall you will, as often as not, be thrown with your head lower down the hill than your ski. You should then lift your ski round until they are below you. Place them horizontal to the slope, hold your sticks horizontally on your uphill side, and get up.

Snow-Ploughing

The beginner should never use his sticks for
reducing his speed. It is quite easy to reduce
the speed either by snow-ploughing, stemming,
or the swings. Of these snow-ploughing is a
very effective method, provided the slope is

Side-Stepping

not too steep and the snow is not too deep.
The position assumed by the ski is a 'V-shaped'
position, with the vertex of the 'V'' pointing
down the slope. Push the legs wide apart and
keep the knees unbent. Distribute the weight
equally on both ski and keep the feet level,
pointing the ski inwards at the toes until the
tips of the ski nearly touch each other; the tips,
however, should not cross. Turn the ski on to

their inside edges and lean well forward down the slope. The wider the angle between the ski and the more the ski are edged, the greater will be the breaking power. This position is most used on roads and hard-beaten snow. It is very difficult to hold in soft deep snow. When travelling fast it is not possible to pull up speedily by this method, and on really steep ground the Telemark stem is far preferable. It is, however, most important for the beginner to practise this position until he can hold it with perfect ease, as the snow-plough is the key to the stemming turn. You should try it on the practice ground where the snow is well beaten down, and you should persevere until you can regulate your speed to a nicety.

Stemming

The stemming position is more or less equivalent to a half snow-plough. It is perhaps the most generally useful of all ski manoeuvres. It is the safest and surest way of preventing the speed from increasing on steep and difficult ground. Point the upper ski down the slope in the direction in which you wish to run, and keep the lower ski nearly horizontal. The tip of the lower ski should be close to but slightly in front of the upper ski (This, as Lieutenant Bilgeri shows, is sounder than the old plan of keeping the lower ski slightly in the rear of the upper ski). You are now in the stemming position, and if you put your weight on the top ski and hold the stemming ski nearly flat against the slope, you will move down the slope with very little breaking effect. In order to weight the upper ski you must bend your knee and crouch down on the upper ski, extending the other leg. The steeper the slope and the steeper the traverse you are making, the more you must crouch on the upper ski, until you are almost sitting on it. If, however, you wish to reduce your speed, straighten your upper leg, throw your weight on to the lower ski, edge it, and you will soon come to a stop. If you wish to proceed at a slow and steady pace without stopping, you can regulate your speed by weighting the upper ski when the pace is too slow, and the lower ski when the pace becomes too fast. The great difficulty in learning this manoeuvre is to get the tips of the ski into their proper relative positions. Stemming should be learned on practice grounds where the snow has been beaten down. This movement should be thoroughly mastered, as it is the foundation of the stemming turn.

Side-Slipping

The beginner is often nervous when the ski begin to side-slip, but the expert makes great use of the side-slip for getting down difficult ground, and often relies on it for helping out the Christiania swing. It is simpler when running on steep ground than stemming, and less exhausting.

Run with your ski in the normal position for traversing a slope, pointing slightly downhill. Flatten them against the slope and slip sideways. Then run a little way in the normal position and again side-slip. The side-slip may also be made use of for an uphill turn. If you wish to stop at the end of a run without pulling up gradually by stemming, flatten your ski against the slope and throw your weight on to your heels. This will make your ski turn uphill. This movement is the foundation of the Christiania and is the best way of learning that swing. It is a far simpler method of stopping when traversing a steep slope than stemming. You should be careful not to lean into the hill, as any conscious effort to lean inwards is bound to result in a fall towards the slope. In all side-slipping it is often a good plan to edge the ski slightly for reasons explained in the following paragraph.

In various movements the ski have to be edged, and it is of importance to grasp

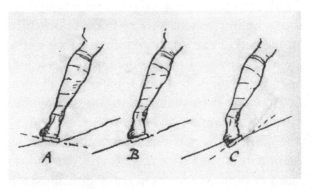

Diagram 2

the general principle of edged ski. Roughly speaking, the ski ought always to be edged so that the line of the leg from the knee to the foot is at right angles to the blade of the ski, as in A in the diagram.* B and C show an awkward strained position in which the ski are not edged sufficiently. In many manoeuvres it is necessary to side-slip and to hold the ski nearly flat against the snow, but if the ski are held quite flat any slight projection, such as a hard lump of snow, will strike the edge of the ski, and the shock will be distinctly felt. If, however, the ski are slightly edged, the shock will come on the sole of the ski and will make little difference. In all turns and swings the ski should be held in what I shall call the 'normal edged position', so that the leg from the knee downwards is at right angles to the blade of the ski, as in A in the diagram.

It is obvious that the beginner who has mastered the various movements will be able to go on a run with considerable safety. He will be able to check his speed by stemming or side-slipping, but he will have to make a kick turn at the end of every tack to join one tack to the next. This will waste considerable time. He will therefore require to learn some downhill turn. It is possible to make continuous downhill turns by stemming, by the Telemark, and by the Christiania. Of these three methods, the stemming turn is the most generally useful on hard or difficult snow. On really difficult snow the other two turns are not easy or advisable, whereas the stemming turn can always be used excepting in deep soft snow, where, fortunately, the Telemark is quite easy. The disadvantage of the stemming turn is that it cannot be done at a great pace, but complete mastery of it is essential for any ski-runner who wishes to go in for Alpine skiing.

To learn it you should find some practice ground where the snow has been well beaten down, and should try the movement first of all on an easy slope. I advise you to practise it with a stick in each hand, as you will have to carry sticks on tour. Many people learn these turns and swings without sticks, and seem handicapped when they have to do them on a mountain carrying their sticks. On no account use a single stick, as you will be tempted to lean on it when turning. The key to the stemming turn is the snow-plough position. If you run downhill snow-ploughing, you have only to throw your weight on the right ski and you will turn uphill to the left. If you are running across the hill in the normal position with the lower foot leading and the hill on your right (for a downhill turn to the right you start with the hill on your left, and substitute right for left and left for right with the following directions), you should first reduce your pace to about six miles an hour by stemming, but take care not to turn uphill. The next step is to straddle your feet as far apart as possible and edge both your ski inwards in the normal-edged position. Keep your knees as straight as possible throughout, and throw your weight on to the top ski. You will gradually swing round until you are pointing down the hill in the ordinary snow-plough position. This is, perhaps, the most difficult part of the turn, and you will completely spoil your turn if you show any tendency to hang back, or to let your knees distinctly bend, or to alter the relative position of your ski. Keep your legs firmly straight; try to pretend that you are diving to the bottom of the slope. Weight the outside ski, and you will gradually swing round.

The beginner is apt to spoil his turn by the following faults: He puts too much weight on the inside ski and allows the ski to run together too soon, or he hangs back when pointing downhill. Note that if you turn to the left the right foot leads throughout. This fact Zdarsky and Rickmers have overlooked. In their diagrams the right foot is made to fall behind at the end of the turn. The beginner is very fond of prodding furtively at the slope. It is far better to try to keep the sticks absolutely clear of the snow.

The method of making the stemming turn by lifting the inner ski has been called the 'Stemmiania' a 'portmanteau' word combining 'Stemming' and 'Christiania'. This method of making the stemming turn is far preferable to the other, and no one who has learnt it is likely to go back to the older style. When you are pointing downhill in the normal snow-plough position you should give a vigorous push-off from the left on to the right leg and lift the loft ski, bringing it smartly down parallel to the other. By this means you are able to make a much sharper and neater turn. The difficulty is to lay down the inside ski exactly parallel to the other. If they cross, you are almost sure to be thrown, and are likely to be if they merely diverge.

'Stemmiark'. This even more unlovely 'portmanteau' might be used as a nickname for the following movement. In deep snow it is often useful to let the stemming turn finish as a Telemark. As you begin to come round throw your weight on to the outside ski and bend your knee, taking as much weight as possible off the back ski and letting it fall to the rear as in the Telemark position. (See also the directions for doing the Telemark swing.)

I recommend the beginner to read Caulfeild's extremely clever analysis of the dynamics of the Telemark and Christiania swings. Subsequent writers are bound to be greatly indebted to him.

Telemark Swing

The Telemark swing is chiefly useful in deep snow, where it is impossible to make a stemming turn unless you pull yourself round with a stick. The Telemark can be used either for stopping suddenly or for making downhill turns. The great advantage of the Telemark is that it is possible to take it at a much higher speed

Stemming

Snow-Ploughing

than the stemming turn. It is not easy to start a stemming turn if you are going at a greater speed than six or eight miles an hour, whereas you can swing round with the Telemark at any speed provided the snow is deep and good. It is not easy to make a Telemark on the ordinary beaten practice ground. The beginner should select some northern slope with good snow for learning this swing.

Uphill turn to the left. (In the Telemark to the right, substitute left for right and right for left throughout.) Run across the slope with the hill on your left in normal running position. Advance the lower foot and fall into the Telemark position, throwing the weight on the leading ski and bending both knees, but especially the back knee. The whole secret of making the Telemark is to keep the weight well on the leading ski, and if you bend the back knee till your back foot is resting on the points of the toes it will be obviously impossible to get any weight on to the back ski. You are now in a position to begin the swing. You must now turn the leading ski on its inside edge and press its heel sharply downwards and outwards, trying to lift your toes (this last instruction is given by Caulfeild, and is a very useful device ; when you have once got the feel of lifting your toes against the toe-straps you have overcome half the difficulty of the turn). If your ski are properly weighted and the leading ski is turned' on its edge, you will begin to swing uphill and soon come to a stop.

The beginner usually fails through one of the following faults: At the critical moment he throws some weight on to the back ski, but does not lean forward enough—he tends to lean into the slope—and he tries to force the swing by leaning towards the slope and by looking in the direction in which he wishes to go. The whole secret of the turn is not to make any conscious effort to swing inwards, but to trust simply to the proper weighting of the ski, and to look always in the direction you are going at the moment, and not in the direction you wish to go.

The reader who has followed me so far will have discovered that in straight running 'Lean forward' is an excellent motto for the beginner, but not for the expert. Just in the same way, when making the Telemark turns the beginner is well advised not to lean consciously inwards, but the expert who makes the swing at a great pace, and who has overcome the tendency to what may be called a 'funk fall', may perhaps find it necessary to help the swing by a conscious inward lean. As a rule, however, the natural instinct to lean inwards is sufficiently strong to render any conscious effort unnecessary. The beginner should practise this swing swinging across the slope at gradually steeper angles until he can make a very sharp uphill swing from a straight run down a steep slope.

As explained before, the value of continuous downhill Telemark turns lies in the fact that they may be done in deep snow and at a far higher rate of speed than the stemming turn. The downhill Telemark turn is really a combination of two movements. The first thing to do is to manoeuvre your ski so that they are pointing straight downhill; you can then finish the turn by an ordinary uphill Telemark swing. You will have noticed that in making the uphill swing the leading ski is edged in the direction in which you wish to turn; the same is true of the downhill swing. If you are running across the slope with the hill on your right and your ski very nearly horizontal, and you wish to turn round to the left, the first thing to do is to edge the ski in the direction in which you wish to go. In other words, instead of keeping the ski horizontal and therefore edged to the slope, you should gradually flatten the ski, and as you begin to swing round to the left, finish the swing by edging the outside right ski to the left. To begin the turn, slide the uphill ski forward and drop into the Telemark position. Throw your weight on to the toe of the leading foot and flatten the leading ski against the slope by turning in the ankle and knee. The leading ski will then begin to turn downhill. When it is pointing straight downhill you can finish the turn by the ordinary uphill swing; that is to say, you will transfer your weight from your toe to your heel and complete the swing as above. The faster you are travelling at the moment you begin the swing, the sooner you must change your weight from the toe to the heel. Throughout the turn be careful to keep the line of the leading leg from the knee to the ankle perpendicular and well over the leading ski. Don't try to force this swing by leaning in the direction in which you wish to go, but rely simply on the correct weighting and edging of the ski.

The Telemark stem, which I believe Lieutenant Bilgeri invented, is an excellent way of taking a steep narrow stretch of ground. Though the position looks difficult, it is quite easy to hold, and the manoeuvre is easy to learn. All you have to do is to kneel on the back ski and put the other ski round in front of and at right angles to the back ski. The back ski will then be pointing straight down the slope, and the front ski will lie right across the slope. Naturally enough, this position gives a very powerful stemming action. It is not easy to fall into this position when running at any speed, nor can you hold it at a speed greater than three to four miles an hour. Its chief advantage is for short, steep, narrow stretches of soft snow. Herr Björnstad, the well-known Norwegian runner, criticises this position on the ground that it is tiring to hold, that the balance is insecure, and that any falls that result from it are apt to be rather unpleasant. I can only agree with the last part of this criticism. The chief difficulty I have found is that the back knee slips off the ski into the snow and gives one a nasty jar. This can be obviated by fixing permanently a small shaped leather pad on the ski into which the knee would just fit.

It is easy to discover useful variations of the Telemark stem, such as the half Telemark stem, when running across a slope. I refer the reader who knows German to Lieutenant

Bilgeri's excellent book on skiing, in which this manoeuvre is fully discussed.

Christiania Swing

Perhaps the most clever chapter in Caulfeild's book is that which analyses the Christiania swing. He divides the Christiania into the 'jerked' and the 'steered' Christiania.

The Christiania which he teaches is started and partly carried through by weighting one foot only. I don't think that this is the best way of making a Christiania, for the following reason. The Christiania which I shall explain is made by weighting both feet, and its great advantage is this, that, owing to the fact that two feet are used instead of one, it is a quicker and stronger turn than the Telemark or Caulfeild's Christiania, the position is far less constrained, and the balance is therefore easier. Caulfeild's method of teaching the Christiania has certain advantages. It is rather easier to do in deep snow, and downhill Christianias are very difficult by the method which I explain; but, on the other hand, in deep snow it is far simpler to do a Telemark than a Christiania, and downhill Christianias are of very little practical importance on any but moderate slopes.

The best way of learning the Christiania swing has already been explained under side-slipping. I would advise the beginner to run across the slope on fairly hard snow at a moderate angle, and get the feel of the Christiania by weighting his heels and turning sharply uphill. Christiania swing to the left. Hold the ski well together. Advance the left ski a little ahead of the other, weight both ski evenly, lean well forward, bend the knees, and thrust round the heels of both ski outwards to the right; at the same time swing your body round rapidly, but don't try to force the turn by leaning in towards the slope at the beginning of the swing, though if you are doing the swing fast in soft snow you will have to lean in considerably towards the end of the swing. The ski must be edged throughout. At the finish you will be leaning towards the slope with your ski well together, but on hard snow it is quite permissible to make this swing with the ski well apart, as in the illustrations. It is quite possible to make downhill swings by this method, but, unlike the Telemark, the downhill Christiania is of very little practical use, for, as I have said, in deep snow it is much easier to make a Telemark, and on hard snow the 'stemmiania' is much more reliable as a downhill turn than the Christiania.

The uphill Christiania swing is a most valuable manoeuvre, and one which the beginner should learn as soon as possible. It is easiest on hard snow with a shallow layer of about one or two inches of new snow. It is the best uphill swing on hard wind-swept snow, and can also be done, though less easily, in deep snow. It is a very powerful swing and is, on the whole, rather safer than the Telemark.

Jumping

My own experience of jumping is very small. I did begin to jump a few winters ago, but my accident has prevented me from taking it up again. I strongly advise the beginner to start jumping as soon as possible. Englishmen have neglected this branch of the sport, and the average beginner looks upon jumping as something entirely beyond his powers. It is, to a certain extent, true that jumping is of no practical value on tour, as the occasions on which one can take a jump on tour without carefully examining the run-out are very few and far between. On the other hand, jumping improves the balance and the dash of the runner as no other form of skiing can do. Touring on ski gives one a certain control and steadiness, but a single afternoon on the jumping field improves one's balance and one's dash more than a dozen full-day runs.

I refer the beginner to the excellent chapter on jumping in Mr Richardson's book *The Ski-runner*. Mr Richardson is the leading English runner, and has done more for the sport in England than anybody else. The beginner should practise the movements of jumping on an ordinary slope, and until he has carefully mastered the 'sats' he should not attempt to jump even from the humblest of take-offs. When he has got this movement correct he should try on small jumps, and gradually work up to the crowning glory of a big jump.

A small jump may be built on almost any hill with a northern or eastern aspect, provided, of course, that the hill is fairly smooth. All you have to do is to thrust a few planks or branches, or a log of wood, into the side of the hill, and pile on snow above it to form a platform which merges gently into the hill above. This is the take-off, and should be about two or three feet high. The take-off should point slightly downwards, as it is far easier for the beginner to stand if the slopes above and below the take-off are more or less of the same steepness. The steeper the hill the better, but I suggest twenty-five degrees is enough for a beginner; if the snow is new and soft it should be stamped below the take-off so as to prevent a nasty pitch forward. The jumper should run down towards the platform in the normal position. About ten yards from the edge of the platform he should stoop down, keeping his knees together and well forward, and crouch till he can touch his ankles with his hands; he should then draw his hands right back and make the 'sats' by the following method: Without raising the heels or moving the feet and legs below the knee, swing your arms forward and upward and straighten yourself smartly until your body and thighs are in a line with the lower part of the legs; you will then, if you have moved from the knees only, be leaning well forward. You should try to imagine that your heels are glued to the ski, and on no account make any attempt to jump from the toes. On completing the 'sats' hold the erect position during the flight through the air; your ski should be parallel to the slope. Just before landing press the knees together, and as you feel your feet touch the snow, and not before, drop into the Telemark position. The moment you feel steady straighten up again, finish your run in the normal position, and swing or jump round.

These directions are taken from Caulfeild's book, which treats the subject far more fully than I am prepared to do, as my experience of jumping is small. None the less, I am fully convinced that jumping is far too much neglected among English runners, and that it is perhaps the best of all methods of acquiring real skill in skiing.

3

Touring and Mountaineering on Ski

Beginners on Tour

The beginner will soon leave the practice ground for his first long tour. Most novices make the mistake of attempting too much. They are persuaded by well-meaning but mistaken friends to join a party on a longish day. Fifteen hundred feet is the outside limit for the first experiment beyond the practice ground, but it is no unusual thing for a novice to try a climb nearer 3000 feet than 2000 feet above the hotel. If the expedition makes a reasonably early start no great harm will be done. The novice will be tired, and if he spoils the run for the more expert members of the party they have only themselves to thank, as they should have realised what they were undertaking. The novice can usually manage the climb all right, and the fact that the party keeps together on the ascent often deceives him into believing that he will not keep people back on the return journey. He has discovered that he can run down steep slopes on the practice ground without falling, and he imagines that he will not fall unduly often on tour. He does not realise that it is one thing to control your ski on a slope with whose gradient you are familiar, and quite another proposition to avoid repeated falls when you are wearied with a long climb and puzzled by unknown country.

Those who lead a party mainly composed of beginners should realise their responsibilities. They should see that their rucksack contains some spare gloves, first-aid appliances, a spare tip, enough food, and a lantern. The last important item is usually neglected. I have more than once had to make a forced descent in the dark owing to a novice claiming more than his fair share of falls, and the lantern which I did not take would have proved very useful.

A careful and sympathetic man can do wonders with a novice on tour. I have seen ski-runners lose their temper and become mildly despondent when a novice falls five times in as many minutes. This is bad form and bad mountaineering. To sulk on a mountain is the

Half-way Through the Stemming Turn

unforgivable sin, and the man who cannot meet
with frolic welcome the small annoyances of a
tour had better stay behind. Besides, the poor
novice does not fall to amuse himself, and he
is quite as anxious as you are to get home in
time for dinner. If you wearily invoke heaven
when he tumbles and loudly speculate on the
possibility of being benighted, you will knock
20 per cent, off the weaker brother's pluck.

On the other hand, wonders can be done with patience and sympathetic nursing. You should run on about 30 yards ahead of the beginner, and set him a nice, easy gradient across steep slopes. You should then stop and encourage him. You cannot insist too often and too sternly on the necessity for leaning forwards and out from the slope, for the moment he begins to tire his nerve will go, and funk falls, backwards and inwards, will be the result. Judicious praise will work miracles, but you must be very stern with him when he falls backwards. Here kindness is misplaced mercy. On the other hand, when he takes an honest forward toss pick him up and pat him on the back.

The reader who is not a novice may think that I have harped enough on these early trials, but the first few tours are of great importance, and if he acts on these hints he will soften the path of the troubled beginner. I have so often seen a man go to pieces at the beginning of a run and pick up surprisingly under careful coaching that I have insisted, perhaps unduly, on the value of consideration in the leader.

I have often found that a ten minutes' rest, coupled with a little food, puts new life into a party. This is especially the case when the situation is serious and the moral of the party is in danger. If you are caught by night or mist your first inclination is to hurry, but a ten minutes' rest in which to feed and consider the situation calmly is an excellent investment of time, however valuable.

What to do in Case of a Collapse

If a man breaks down hopelessly, giving him a line will not be enough. In this case you should put your arm firmly round his waist and hold him up. You will be surprised to find how easily you can take slopes in this position. The tension of your arm should vary as little as possible, and the two ski-runners should form for purposes of balance one solid body. This sounds a difficult manoeuvre, but it is almost as easy to run without falling in this position as when skiing alone. I have seen it done with great success. If you are taller than the other man you should keep below him when crossing a slope and, of course, you will have to stop and do a kick turn at the end of every traverse.

Ladies on Tour

Skiing is admirably adapted to the physique of the average woman. It does not involve sudden spurts of ferocious energy. The labour of the ascent is not concentrated into brief spasms of effort, but is evenly spread over a long interval. If the lady runner has mastered the correct style, her skiing will be free and effortless. The sport does not involve ungainly attitudes. A lady playing hockey is a strangely unaesthetic object, but the same woman on ski may easily prove more graceful and attractive than in any other role. Ladies, more often than not, possess the nerve and dash essential to brilliant ski-running, and there is very little reason why they should require the traditional 'half' in competitions. Last year Miss Maitland, perhaps the neatest of lady ski-runners, beat some strong candidates in an open competition for style and secured the first prize.

Ladies have, moreover, the stamina for severe expeditions. On mountaineering, of course, they are quite outclassed by men, and when we hear of ladies transposing 'the most difficult climb in the Alps' into an 'easy day for a lady', it is well to remember that every expedition made by a lady is led by a man. Till ladies begin to carry out severe guideless climbs without masculine assistance, they cannot be considered in the same class with a good man mountaineer. None the less they make very good seconds on the rope. As a rule they show greater pluck and give less trouble than men when things go wrong, chiefly because they retain to the last a touching, if misplaced, confidence in the male members of the party. I have been in more than one nasty experience in the Alps with ladies, and I have been profoundly thankful for their courage and unfailing cheerfulness.

Where ladies so often fail is in want of imagination and want of thought. Without wishing to intrude on controversial ground, I think most mountaineers would agree that women have less imagination than men. This acts both ways. It is often an advantage, as it blinds them to the worst aspects of a dangerous situation. A man can translate the statement that a night on the mountain is a painful ordeal into practical terms of sensation. Women don't seem to have the same power, and I have more than once heard a girl express with real conviction her ambition to go through the experience of being benighted. And their lack of imagination shows itself in other ways. A man knows as a living fact and not as a mere academic supposition that though he may be packing his rucksack after breakfast he will undoubtedly feel hungry higher up. A girl in similar circumstances decides that she has lost for ever the sensation of hunger, and will cheerily assure you that three biscuits, a bar of chocolate, and an apple will suffice for an eight-hour run. Similar argument will convince her that spare gloves and a woollen helmet are unnecessary additions to her sack. Later they either turn to you for assistance or, from a foolish striving after a consistency which no one expects from their sex, decline food and garments, thus risking faintness and frostbite. A man realises when he is in danger through exhaustion. He knows when the solid supply of normal energy is depleted, and he realises when he begins to draw on his nervous energy. Nervous energy is a valuable asset, and will carry a man through a storm long after his ordinary strength has vanished. But no man who is not a fool will drain this valuable reserve fund excepting in cases of necessity. Women, on the other hand, never differentiate between capital and income. They do not know when they are done, or if they do know it, they will persevere from a false sense of pride, or from the dread of spoiling the day for other people. All this is quite admirable in a way. One extends a qualified admiration to the most perverted forms of pluck, though one resents the courage due to that lack of imagination on which I have commented. If a girl realised the plight of her friends in the event of a breakdown, she would be loth to spoil their present enjoyment and would frankly admit that she had attempted something beyond her power. And often this overtaxing of nervous strength will result, if not in immediate collapse, in dangerous symptoms weeks later. Lastly, ladies should realise that mere stupidity has caused more than one perilous collapse above the snowline, and that a girl who starts for a tour when she is in bad health is—to put it mildly—showing a selfish lack of consideration for the rest of the party, and a criminal neglect of essential precautions.

I gladly admit that many lady mountaineers and ski-runners set an admirable example to men. They do their fair share of the work and are properly indignant if a man offers to adjust their bindings or carry their ski. Also they carry a rucksack. Such ladies are a welcome addition to any party, and are fit for serious winter mountaineering.

There are, of course, cases where a man gladly accepts the responsibility of shepherding less capable ladies. If a girl who is not strong shows pluck and enthusiasm, you may willingly carry her ski and her provisions in order to bring tours, otherwise beyond her, well within her reach. And, of course, a man always expects to carry the spare tip, rope, lantern, &c., and something more than his fair share of the provisions. But, none the less, a girl who habitually climbs with men should strive to be as independent as possible of masculine assistance and should regard it as a point of honour to start properly equipped for every emergency.

I do not feel myself qualified to offer any advice on dress, and I refer the lady ski-runner to the most excellent chapter contributed by Mrs Rickmers to her husband's book. Mrs Rickmers, incidentally, is herself a striking illustration of the best type of lady ski-runners, and to this day 1 still blush at the memory of her reply when I offered to carry her share of the lunch. Perhaps she will pardon me for quoting from her advice on the subject of dress.

If one is going in seriously for skiing it is really worth while to get a good costume for the purpose ... to be useful and at the same time becoming it should consist of a coat, skirt, and knickerbockers, all of the same strong material, to which snow will not stick. The coat should be double-breasted, loose, and not too short, for the secret of making a satisfactory masculine costume for a woman lies in concealing the lines of her figure . . . the pockets should be large enough . . . The knickerbockers should be most carefully cut. The tight riding breeches so much affected by men are not becoming to a woman's figure, tending to give her a knock-kneed appearance. Wherever there is actual tendency to knock knees, however slight, the knickers should be made to hang a little at the knees. This can be done without giving them any semblance to bloomers. The skirt should be short and as light as possible, so that it can be carried in one's rucksack and donned and doffed when necessary. To make movement easy when it is worn over the knickerbockers the front breadth might be lined with silk. As to what is worn under the coat individual taste must decide. Some ladies will prefer a sweater, some a flannel shirt. The point to remember is that the coat or some wind-proof garment (such as a jacket of impregnated silk) must accompany one on tour, and that no amount of extra sweaters can take its place.

Mrs Rickmers recommends a simple coiffure on which the cap sets firmly, and as for headgear ladies should carry in their sacks a woollen helmet and a silk scarf for severe cold. In normal weather they can please themselves. The boots must be good and several sizes too large. No one wnll attempt to deduce the size of a lady's foot from the appearance of her skiing boots. In this, as in the rest of the outfit, vanity is an expensive failing.

I live in hopes that common-sense will work downwards from the snowline to the valley, and that knickerbockers may soon become as common in Swiss valleys as they are now in club huts. The ladies of the Black Forest have defied fashion. There seems no intrinsic reason why knickers should not be as becoming as a skirt. If a skirt must be carried, it seems odd that it cannot be made to serve some useful purpose when discarded high up on the mountains. I suppose the suggestion of a combination coat and cape could emanate only from an ignorant male, but some such method as employing the skirt during, say, a cold luncheon hour would mitigate the irritation of this stupid garment.

Mountaineering on Ski

Ski-runners may roughly be divided into two classes: those to whom the actual skiing is everything, and those who are mainly interested in skiing as an aid to winter mountaineering. The latter class are just as anxious as the former to get good running, but they are willing to compromise and sacrifice something to the odd fancy for getting to the top of a peak. I confess that the man who confines himself to comparatively easy tours gets better value as far as skiing pure and simple is concerned than the mountaineer. First-class snow is the exception, not the rule, above 10,000 feet. The wind and the sun wreak great havoc, and all forms of wind-swept and patchy snow are abominable. The average running on a glacier is quite fair, but the powder snow—a snow to dream of—is hardly ever met with.

In any centre worthy of the name there is a run of some 3000 feet which gives excellent skiing throughout its length. It is rare to get 6000 feet of good running, though the descent from the Oberaarjoch to Guttanen or from the Jungfrau Joch to Gampel afford some 9000 feet of fine skiing.

To me the most enjoyable of all forms of skiing is the crossing of passes. This is the simplest and most primitive use of the ski. It is in harmony with the original employment of ski as a help to communication between snowbound valleys. And no man who is a traveller at heart will be content with the life of big hotels. So many English people only change the position of their bodies when they go abroad. Their minds remain for ever in England, and they translate their local environment when they journey. They are unhappy if their hotels contain 'foreigners', such as, for instance, the inhabitants of the country in which they are staying, and I have heard a man bitterly complain of a certain German hotel that it was full of Germans. Somehow that does not seem the proper spirit of the traveller. The man who is a wanderer at heart will eschew the company of his own countrymen. He will try to learn something of the people among whom he travels, and for him the Swiss will not be a nation of hotel-keepers.

The man who wishes to get the best out of the Alps and the best out of his ski will wander from valley to valley with his kit on his back. He will love the long hours of gradual ascent to some tantalising skyline whose secrets he has only guessed at from the map. Geography will become a vital reality as each section of the Siegfried associates itself with living memories. He will live a simple, primitive life, passing from club huts to lonely hamlets, and instead of the vulgar bathos of the return to the hotel he will wind up a day on the untroubled heights over a glass of wine with the *cure*. He will see something of that industrial life which is as old as the hills that govern its unchanging cycle, and his Alpine memories will be bound up with the thought of goodwill from stranger hands, of long evenings beneath the stained timbers of some wayside chalet where he had asked, and not asked in vain, for shelter and food.

Planning out a Tour

In deciding the choice of a route various considerations come into play. Slopes facing north or east should always give good running under normal conditions, whereas on slopes facing south and west the snow becomes crusty and very tricky. Unfortunately the most gradual slopes are usually found facing south or east, for the simple reason that the slopes which get the most sun are those which have been the most cultivated; moreover, in the course of time, the sun has smoothed down the asperities on southern and western slopes, while the hill-sides on which the sun shines with less vigour tend to be rough and uneven. However, in most centres, it is possible to find northern and eastern slopes which are in every way suited for skiing.

The Siegfried map, intelligently used, gives an excellent clue to the nature of unknown country. The interval between every two contour lines represents a vertical height of 30 metres, and where these lines are close together steep ground is to be expected. The ski-runner should purchase the maps of the district which he wishes to explore, and make a special note of those slopes on which the contours are wide apart and evenly spaced. Trees and forests are marked on the map, and should be avoided as far as possible, though it is easy to carry this principle to excess, as larch forests sometimes give very good running, larch trees as a rule growing less densely than pine trees.

Finally the ski-runner should not place too much reliance on mere guide-books, or on guides who only know the conditions in summer. The conditions are totally altered in winter, and he should consult such ski guides as he can lay hold of. The Alpine Ski Club have published a guide to the Western Oberland from the Kandersteg to Villars, which is the first of a series that should prove very useful

(The price of this guide-book has been reduced to 2s).

It is a good plan to have a rough list of outfit, which may be made up from Chapter II of this book, and to consult it before starting so as to see that no essential portion of the outfit is left behind. The leader of the party should see that a spare ski tip and some bandages are carried. Such emergency portions of the outfit should be divided amongst the party, If there are any ladies in the party it is advisable to see that they are carrying at least two pairs of gloves and some protection for their ears and chin, as ladies are apt to be very casual about kit, and to trust to the male members of the party to come to the rescue if the weather turns cold.

The Climb

The first part of the climb will usually be on a road or path. You can either drag your ski along the path with string or carry them. The best way of carrying the ski is to place them sole to sole, and carry them across your shoulder. It is a good plan to divide the weight by resting them on a ski stick carried across the other shoulder. If there is a path for a part of the ascent the reader should always choose this, as it is about 20 per cent quicker to walk up the path on foot than to climb adjacent slopes on ski. When the path stops, the party will put on their ski, and their sealskins if they

The Telemark Position

have not already done so. The leader should
choose a gradient suited to the needs of the
weakest member of the party. If anyone has
not got sealskins he must be careful to choose
a gradient which the whole party can climb
without slipping back. Every member of the
party should be on the look-out to observe the
characteristics of the country through which
they are passing, and to make mental notes of
any difficulties for the homeward run. Mark
specially the presence of half-concealed fences
and ground which steepens suddenly, as these
slopes present a very different appearance from

above than from below. You should turn round pretty regularly in order to have the view from above. If there is a choice of route for the final pull it is usually better to follow a windswept ridge, carrying the ski, than to climb up sheltered slopes on ski. Slopes should be followed on the east in preference to north slopes if the snow is so crusty that it is easy to walk up with the ski on one's shoulders. Let me repeat that walking on hard snow is always faster than climbing up soft snow on ski. It is advisable to lunch a little way below the summit provided you can get a sunny place, as it is a pity to start down on the ski run feeling cold, and the exercise of climbing from the lunching place to the top restores the circulation.

The Descent

When you are beginning the run home you should wax your ski if the snow is at all sticky or likely to be sticky lower down. Remember what I have said about northern and eastern slopes, 'with this proviso, that even on southern slopes you may get good running by choosing an artful route. If a southern slope is broken up into ridges you may often get good snow on the eastern slopes of a southern ridge. A good example of this is the Petersgrat. I crossed this pass nearly three years ago, and endured vile running. The Petersgrat faces south-east. Our guides took us down the western slopes of the Tellispitzen, which faces very nearly due west, and on which we had in consequence very bad snow. If they had taken us down the eastern slopes of a ridge which runs parallel with the Tellispitzen (the Grindelspitzen) we should have had perfect running to the Fafler Alp. If the snow is in good condition there will be no difficulty, but the snow is very often entirely ruined. You will get patches of bad snow alternating with sticky pockets of soft snow, and the only way to take such a slope is to run it in Telemark position or to crouch down very low on one ski, leaning well back.

On a dull day it is not easy to distinguish the gradient. If the sky is at all overcast all inequalities vanish and it is quite easy to go over a 15 feet (or 150 feet, for that matter) drop without realising until it is too late that the slope has changed. Try to put into practice the various turns and swings you have learned, using downhill Telemarks in deep soft snow, and downhill stemming turns on hard wind-swept snow, stopping suddenly by means of the Christiania, or less often by means of the Telemark.

In breakable crust it is possible to make Telemark or Christiania swings provided the crust is not too deep, but as a rule you will, if the crust is bad, have to be content with traversing across the hill, and changing your direction by means of kick turns. The expert can jump round, but this manoeuvre is neither safe nor easy. On a small mountain you should risk a few falls by trying experiments. Never go on a small tour without making a conscious effort to raise the speed limit at which you feel comfortable. When, however, you are hours away from the nearest hotel caution, perhaps, is the more reasonable and wiser plan. 'High mountains are not the place to try experiments, or to show off pretty tricks' (Hoek). If the ground steepens suddenly and you cannot see the slopes below the bend, you should never run straight to the point where the ground steepens, but you should approach it on a curve, and be ready at any moment to swing uphill. You will thus prevent yourself from dropping over a precipice.

Skiing in the high Alps

Skiing in the high Alps is rather a different matter. The outfit is more complicated, and I would refer the reader to Chapter 2, in which this question is thoroughly discussed. The members of the party should be good steady ski-runners who are not likely to keep the party back by falling or to risk a night on the mountain by breaking their legs.

At least one member of the party should know something about the mountains in summer, should understand the anatomy of the mountainside, and be able to form a rough guess at the type of ground that lies beneath the snow, whether it is scree or grass, rocky slabs or glacier.

Mountaineering on ski is not much more arduous than summer climbing, provided the conditions are perfect. The days are, of course, shorter in winter, and this is the most serious obstacle. The times taken, however, are much the same in winter as in summer. What is lost on the ascent is gained on the descent. Moreover, the ascent, though longer, is less laborious. In winter one climbs at a slower speed. The advance is deliberate. In summer the angle of ascent is constantly changing and is often steep. In winter one climbs in long zigzags at a constant angle. The ski, acting as shields, save the feet from footsoreness, and the pitiless stony mule path is unknown. The cold is often negligible. During a six-day glacier tour we were never inconvenienced. The guides had a siesta on the snow at a height of 11,000 feet, whilst on the summit of the Finsteraarhorn it was possible to strip in the sun. Long periods of 'inverted temperature' prevail for days together, so that rock ridges with a south aspect are warm, dry, and as easy to climb as in summer.

As to the difficulty of first-class tours, let me assure the novice that if he has had three full weeks of practice he should be able to tackle any of the normal winter climbs. He will be surprised at the ease with which he defeats the average big peak. People who have never been up a mountain often imagine that the ordinary Alpine peak is a succession of terrific precipices with the scantiest of holds. Let me assure them that the main routes up, let us say, the Finsteraarhorn, Eiger, or Matterhorn present no technical difficulties to the second on the rope. The rocks met with are of the type that can be climbed by the light of Nature, and there are few men for whom their first big peak has not proved disappointingly easy. Rock climbing as practised in the Dolomites, the Chamounix aiguilles, or our own Welsh and Cumberland cliffs is a fine art calling for exceptional nerve and resource, but the rough scrambling that characterises the ordinary route up a respectable Alpine peak is by no means an alarming proposition. A man with a good head could make short work of it without previous experience, so long as he had a watchful guide and a stout rope as an insurance against mistakes. Ice is another matter, and a long exposed ice slope will try the nerves of most novices until they have learned to stand well out from their steps. Here, however, crampons will simplify matters, and ice slopes are not often tackled in winter. An able-bodied man who can ski without falling, let us say, more than twice in 1000 feet, who can pass any third-class test with something to spare, who is possessed of a good head, sound wind, and average endurance, can tackle with confidence any of the Oberland peaks. He must engage good guides, and his guides will see that his climbing is on south arêtes, which should prove no harder in winter than in summer. A man who has a weak head may still attempt the great glacier passes without rashness. Of course, if bad weather is encountered the climber will need all the reserve pluck and strength that he is likely to possess, but the climber who meets with bad weather in the high Alps is unlucky or very foolish.

Perfect conditions are for the summer climber an ideal, for the winter mountaineer almost a *sine qua non*. In summer one may attack many mountains when the conditions are far from perfect. A night out is then often merely an unpleasant experience. In winter it is otherwise. The snowstorm and the north wind are fraught with the greatest danger, whilst to be benighted in January involves the probability of fatal results.

The possibility of small accidents is greatly increased by the addition of a new factor: the speed of the descent. To the normal dangers of mountaineering is added the risk of fracturing above by a skiing tumble. And if the possibilities of an accident are increased the accident itself is far more serious than in summer. In July a wounded man might well spend the night on the rocks without succumbing. He could scarcely do so in January. A party containing two guides and three amateurs just managed, with the aid of two peasants, to carry home a ski-runner who had broken his leg on the Zanfleuron Glacier. Three men in a party is the irreducible minimum for high mountaineering in winter, and even three are by no means over secure. Again, in winter the danger area is much more diffused. In summer a child could ascend the Faulhorn alone without danger. In January the Faulhorn can kill like Mont Blanc in July. A man need not climb far to fall foul of an avalanche; it is not so long since ski-runner was overwhelmed and killed within a mile of his hotel. Passes over which one can drive a cow in summer may be death-traps in winter. The Rawyl Pass is only one of many such instances. Herein lies the gravest of winter perils. In summer the novice sticks to the mule path, for public opinion condemns the beginner who crosses the snowline without a guide or an experienced amateur. In winter the tyro learns to shun paths and to wander whenever and wherever there is snow. He tends to glide unconsciously from the practice ground into mountaineering. Now in three weeks a man can master skiing enough to carry him through an expedition provided he has the ordinary endurance and nerve; but years may

Above: Linked Telemarks

Opposite: Finish of Telemark to the Left

be spent in acquiring the elements of avalanche craft. Here, of course, the summer climber starts with a great advantage. His wanderings have taught him something of the anatomy of the mountains, and of the nature of the ground supporting the treacherous snow. For him the danger of the avalanche need not be emphasised, and best of all he has acquired that attitude of constant suspicion without which no ski-runner is safe. He may, of course, as summer guides often do, imagine that he has nothing to learn; that snow in winter at 7000 feet obeys much the same laws as summer snow at 12,000 feet; but in nine cases out of ten he will be a safer companion after a week's skiing than the brilliant runner who has learned his craft on the jumping hill, or in the safe, though difficult, forests of Christiania.

Mountains which can be climbed by the aid of ski may be divided into three classes: (1) Mountains on which ski can be taken to the summit, such as the Wildstrubel, Wildhorn, Zermatt-Breithorn, &c., and, under certain circumstances, Mont Blanc. (2) Mountains on which the last part of the ascent is a rock climb, such as the Grand Combinby the Valsoret arête, Mont Rosa, or the Finsteraarhorn. (3) Mountains on which ski have to be left at the foot of the final ice slopes, such as the Jungfrau.

It is obvious that in order to traverse a mountain it must be approximate to the first of those classes. Rock climbing with ski slung over one's back is a poor sport, and peculiarly difficult. Ski can be hauled up separately over a short, tricky rock climb, or ice slope, but in general passes, and peaks used as passes, must conform to the first of these three classes.

Mountaineers are sometimes divided into those who do their climbs from one centre, and those who wander over passes from village to village. The latter is by far the more enjoyable form of mountaineering on ski, but it is also slightly more difficult. If you return by the same route as you ascend you are able to map out the line of descent and can get a rough idea of the difficulties and dangers. In pass traversing you have no such opportunities, and as a result you must take no chances. Never cross a pass in winter unless you know that the pass has been crossed on ski, or unless someone in the party, guide or amateur, has crossed the ground in summer, and has a rough idea of the difficulties to be faced, or unless the Siegfried very clearly states that no difficulties need be expected. If you are climbing a peak and come to a difficulty you can turn back. If you are pulled up by an unexpected trap on the descent of a pass you must risk it, or re-ascend the pass, and return by the way you came—a very unpleasant alternative. Moreover it is far harder to discover a line from above than from below, as everyone knows who has tried to find the clue to a precipice from its summit. From above slopes are foreshortened, and sudden dips are often invisible. I mention these difficulties not because they detract from what is far the finest form of mountaineering on ski, but simply in order to emphasise the necessity for caution.

Characteristics of the Ski-Running Season

The conditions suitable for skiing in the high Alps have been admirably summed up by Professor Roget in the *Alpine Ski Club Annual*, No. 1, from which I extract the following:

The atmospheric reasons which help to determine the proper ski-running months in the high Alps are of a meteorological description, which are connected mainly with the temperature. We shall begin by giving our thought a paradoxical expression, as follows: it is a mistake to talk of winter at all in connection with the high Alps. According to the time of year, the weather in the Alps is subjected to general rain conditions or to general snow conditions. Under snow conditions, the thermometer is under zero centigrade, and the temperature of the air may range from zero downwards to a very low reading; but the sun is extremely powerful, its force is intensified by the reflection from the snow surface. The temperature of the air in the shade is therefore no clue to the temperature of material surfaces exposed to the rays of the sun. The human frame, under suitable conditions of clothing and exercise, feels and actually is quite warm in the sun, a violent wind being required to approximate the subjective sensations of the body to those usually associated with a cold, damp, and biting winter's day. This is a general characteristic of the so-called Alpine winter, to which must be added an occasional, though perfectly regular, feature, in this, namely, that the Alps may offer, and do offer, every winter instances of inverted temperatures. This name has come to be given to periods which may extend over several days at a stretch, and which are repeated several times during the so-called winter months. These are periods during which the constant temperature of the air (that is, the average temperature by night and by day in the shade) is higher upon the heights than in the plains and valleys. These states of the atmosphere are now daily published in the weather reports quoted by the leading Swiss newspapers, and they are of the utmost value to the ski-runner. As a general principle, the winter sportsman may be sure that, in the proportion in which he rises, he also leaves behind him the winter conditions, as defined, in keeping with their own notions and experience, by the dwellers on plains, on the seaside, or in valleys. When travelling upwards, he reaches a dry air, a hot and bright light, and maybe a higher temperature than prevails in the lower regions of the earth which lie at his feet.

We said a little while ago that in January and February any snowfall improves the floor. In the preceding months the high regions pass gradually from the condition in which they are practicable on foot to those under which they are properly accessible to the ski-runner only. Time must be allowed for the process; till it is completed ski-running is premature and consequently distinctly dangerous. The Alpine huts should not be used as ski-centres before they can be reached on ski, and one should not endeavour to reach them in that manner as long as stones are visible among the snow. The distinctive feature of the ski-runner's floor is that it is free from stones and from holes. The stones should be well buried under several feet of snow and the holes filled up with compressed or frozen snow before the ski-runner makes bold to sally forth, but when they are he may practically go anywhere, and dare anything so far as the ground is concerned, provided he is an expert runner and a connoisseur in the matter of avalanches. Of course, our 'anywhere' applies to ski-grounds only, and our 'anything' means mountaineering as restricted to the uses to which ski may fairly be put.

To sum up, the characteristics of the ski-running season are: Stability of weather; constant dryness of the air; a uniform and continuous running surface; windlessness; a constant temperature from sunrise to sunset; at times a relatively high air temperature; solar light and solar heat, which must not be confused with air temperature, and present an intensity, a duration most surprising to the dweller in plains and on the sea-board; last, but not least, accessibility of the rocky peaks with climbing slopes turned to the sun.

Glaciers

In the old days of skiing it used to be considered that glaciers were safer in winter than in summer. This, however, is not the case. In summer you approach a crevasse at walking speed, and you have ample time to note the small indications in the snow which betray its presence. In winter if you are skiing downhill you are right on top of the crevasse before you realise the danger. True, the great speed at which one travels on ski, and the way in which the -weight is distributed along the whole length of the ski, will enable you to cross bridges which you could not attempt on foot, but on the other hand even the most expert ski-runner occasionally falls, and to fall while crossing a snow bridge may mean a fatal accident. Again, a snow bridge with a depth of three or four inches is often quite secure in summer, as this thickness will be almost entirely ice, but in winter crevasses are covered with bridges of soft wind-swept snow, and whereas six inches would be always safe in summer a bridge 14 feet in depth has broken in winter, and resulted in a fatal accident. So I would say always rope on a glacier, and I say this oven though I have been a great offender in this respect myself. Roped running is rather tedious, and there is a great temptation not to spoil a good run by a rope. On the other hand, a few days' practice on slopes round the hotel with a rope should give the runner sufficient control to be able to run with ease, and to enjoy a long descent on the rope. It is only necessary to practise on mild slopes, as no one would dream of skiing on a really steep glacier. Unfortunately very few ski-runners have the energy to practise rope-running on 'off days', and there is in consequence far too much glacier skiing without a rope. Two or three is the best number for a rope, and there should be at least 20 feet between each runner. The rope should be kept fairly taut, and every man on the rope should be prepared to throw himself down and edge his ski sideways at a moment's notice, the latter manoeuvre giving the most resistance to a pull.

Club Huts

Club huts in winter are fairly comfortable, and almost invariably supplied with wood, for which one is expected to pay a good price, as the labour of carrying up the wood in winter is very severe. It is the duty of the mountaineer to leave a note in the club book as to his destination, so that the search party may have some clue to his whereabouts in the event of an accident.

One of the great dangers of winter mountaineering is the possibility of a long and continued snowstorm which may keep one tied up in a club hut for many days. My guide, Crettex, was once confined for a fortnight in the Concordia. It is very imprudent to begin a big climb without at least three days' emergency provisions. If your provisions run out, and you determine to make a dash through the storm, you should cut up small sticks of wood and plant them at regular intervals of 20 yards as you proceed; this will enable you to get back to the hut if you find it impossible to endure the cold.

Avalanches

The subject of avalanches is peculiarly intricate. Spring and summer avalanches are not difficult to avoid, but our knowledge of 'dry' avalanches is still in the elementary stage. All that can be done here is to indicate a few rough generalities. The only rule is to suspect all slopes above twenty-three degrees in all conditions. If, after a careful survey, you have any doubt turn back or avoid the slope by a detour. Short bits of suspicious ground may be tackled by removing the ski and wading up in a straight line. You are not thus caught with your ski on your feet. On no account divide a suspicious slope by a horizontal cutting. Never rope excepting for short gullies, where some of the party can remain on the rocks and anchor the man who is traversing the dangerous portion. Steep long slopes should always be crossed one at a time. A good plan, as Mr Richardson suggests, is to cross dangerous slopes with the bindings loose, so that if an avalanche starts, it is possible at once to free oneself from one's ski. Another dodge is to carry a Norwegian clasp knife with which to cut the bindings. Once caught in an avalanche both rope and ski will drag you under and prevent your rising to the surface, which can otherwise be done by maintaining a swimming action. Traverse all dangerous slopes as high as possible. If an avalanche starts you are not overwhelmed with snow from above, and have some chance of keeping on the surface. Snow is more dangerous if it rests on glaciers, polished rocks, or grass that is not mown, than on ordinary grass slopes or scree. Rocky slopes, if the rocks are not submerged but get a grip on the snow, are fairly safe. If, however, new snow falls on an old crust which covers the rough substratum, the slope immediately becomes dangerous.

Slopes which narrow down into a trough are far more dangerous than slopes which open out, as the snow is forced into the trough and solidifies much more readily, crushing the unfortunate victim with terrible force. {See the account of Bennen's death on the Haut de Cry quoted at the end of Whymper's *Scrambles amongst the Alps*.)

Suspect gradual slopes if they end in a sudden dip, all slopes beneath rocks laden with new snow, slopes on which you feel the snow settling under you, and other slopes analysed below. It has been suggested that every member of a party should secure to his waist 60 feet or so of coloured rope, which will provide a clue to his temporary grave should he be overwhelmed by an avalanche. This presupposes that the party are wittingly crossing dangerous ground, which, of course, may be the case with a rescue party or in descending a pass. Be most careful when fresh snow is falling, particularly if it is accompanied by wind, and never venture on steep slopes if the Föhn wind prevails.

So much for generalities. The most thorough analysis of avalanches occurs in *Die Gefahren der Alpen* by Zsigmondy-Paulcke. There are valuable chapters on the subject in Mr Rickmers' and Mr Richardson's books, and two articles contain valuable information, viz.

'On Snow Avalanches' by Dr Hoek, in the *Alpine Journal* for February 1907, and 'Two Avalanches', by W. R. Rickmers, in the *Alpine Ski Club Annual* 1909. Avalanches may be classified as follows: Wet-snow avalanches. The *Grundlawinen*. This type of avalanche is least dangerous, because it is easiest to avoid. It occurs when the snow is penetrated by water or drenched by the melting surface. It is experienced very rarely in the higher regions, and is easy to detect. Enormous *Grundlawinen* only fall in spring, and as a rule select well-known sites. The April ski-runner should have no difficulty in learning their tracks. He may, of course, be kept in a club hut and have to wait till night to descend, but in general the ski-runner is not much troubled by the great *Grundlawinen*. Small wet avalanches are, however, fairly common, and constitute a serious danger. A good rule is to mistrust all steep slopes after a fresh fall until the pine trees are free from snow. By this time most of the obvious avalanches will have fallen. Of course, never venture out when the Föhn is blowing, and avoid steep slopes where the sun is beating down on to a layer of fresh snow.

Dry avalanches, or new-snow avalanches are known as *Staublawinen*. These 'wind avalanches' are caused by the disturbance of steep snow lying at a very steep angle. Such snow has a strong internal friction, and in consequence a powerful impact is necessary

Starting a Christiania

Christiania to the Right. Ski Apart.

to start an avalanche. Such an impact is given by a wind, by the fall of a cornice, or by snow sliding off a precipice from above.

Slowly some particles begin to move; they start others; the movement grows swifter. The consequence is a current of air directed towards the valley, a current that itself again moves snow and whirls it up. Finally the whole slope is alive; a destructive whirlwind, laden with enormous quantities of the finest snow, 'the powdery avalanche' roars down, destroying everything in its way. At the foot of the slope most of the snow settles down in a loose, smooth, symmetrical cone, in which the foot sinks deeply. The snow-laden wind rushes onward against the opposite side of the valley. The strongest blast is often some distance above the avalanche; it spares the woods on its own side and uproots those on the opposite slopes. Dry snow is the first condition of this kind of avalanche: the steeper the mountain, the smoother the substratum, the easier it is started. The most liable sites are smooth, grassy slopes with the blades bent down, or grassy snow on which fresh powdery snow has fallen without being congealed. (Dr Hoek, in the *Alpine Journal*, February 1907.)

The wind caused by these avalanches is terribly powerful. On one occasion it destroyed a small inn which the avalanche never touched. It was probably a *Staublawine* that Hans Andersen tried to describe in *The Ice Maiden*.

In cold weather, after snow has fallen, the ski-runner must suspect the existence of these wind avalanches. Unlike the wet avalanches, they have no regular tracks, and the force of the wind may start an avalanche on the opposite side of the valley. 'A blizzard of half an hour's duration may convert into a death-trap a valley which was harmless when the party entered it'. Avoid after fresh snow all along open slopes, especially if they lie under cornices or snow-covered cliffs, and remember that the size of an avalanche is of very little importance. A cubic yard of snow weighs more than half a ton, and a very small slide can kill a man.

The snow slab is by far the most dangerous type of avalanche. The snow, being hard, gives a false impression of security; the slides may occur with a low temperature, possibly many degrees below freezing-point, and several days after a snowfall. Therefore, at all times, at all temperatures, suspect very steep, crusted slopes of snow. These snow shields, or Schnee- Brett as the Germans call them, are nearly always superficial avalanches, consisting of one layer of snow sliding down over a smooth surface of snow. During a strong wind, a quantity of fine snow, of a different consistency from the substratum below, tends to settle on the lee-side of the mountains. Tension results from a variety of causes. As the temperature falls, the new snow surface, densely packed, expands more than the substratum. Sometimes a cavity is formed by the setting of the lower layer. The results are usually much the same. The top layer is in a state of tension; the weight of the ski-runner proves the last straw. The shield cracks in a sharp line, splinters into vast clods, which glide rapidly down, sometimes producing lateral layer breakages, sometimes starting the more normal type of avalanche below. Moreover:

> When speaking of the lee-side we must not think too much of the prevailing winds. In avalanche craft, it means, above all, any side which can accumulate snow when in the lee and keep it when windward. All steep slopes under ridges more or less fulfil this condition, especially when also guarded against lateral blasts by the formation of the ground or rock-screens. Thus the corries (German '*Kar* '), those deep hollows in the mountain flank, are the favourite lair of the avalanche. These dust-bins of the mountain are practically always in the lee, being protected on three sides. A storm blowing into them, be it ever so furious, will raise the snow in great clouds, only to let it fall back again just under the edge.
>
> After a long absence of snowy weather the observant tourist will notice that on the exposed mountains (i.e. above the level indicated by the average height of the passes) most of the slopes, and especially the cupolas and outside curves, are swept clean, while the whitest places are also the steepest. This makes the trap all the more insidious, and the ski-runner is apt, naturally, to follow the line of least resistance, the even flow from the towering sky-line, or the avenue leading up to a pass which crosses the range in some sheltered recess. This larger amount is sufficient alone to explain the great danger on lee-sides, as, for instance, when new falls are accompanied

by wind. But the air currents are also at work during fine weather. The wind-borne material, finely sifted, settles evenly into solid cakes, sometimes of great thick- ness, and is further beaten down and hardened by the hammering action of wind ripples. To this must be added a state of tension caused by thermal changes. Under the influence of the sun's rays the snow bed shrinks and settles through a partial melting process; freezing again, its volume increases, and strong tension is produced which may be said to form vaults of snow. As these vaults are extremely flat and delicately poised (it must not be imagined that they are visible to the naked eye) they cave in under the slightest provocation, turning the slope into a hell of tumbling blocks. On the Patscherkofel, two men, imagining that they had solid ground beneath their feet, sprang one of these mines skilfully laid in the scooped-out basin on the Innsbruck side of the mountain. Fortunately they escaped. I went up next day and found a perfect wilderness of huge blocks, some of them 10 ft. high and solid throughout, being fragments of the snowfloe or cake due to the interrupted growth of one winter. (W.R. Rickmers, *Alpine Ski Club Annual*, 1909.)

Rickmers adds, in his book on skiing:

The snow slab's patchy, partly silky, partly granulated, or rippled, or furrowed surface betrays its origin. On the other hand, one need not fear the regular smooth floor, hard as stone, due to the freezing of soft snow on the southern face after the sun has left it. When wishing to ascertain whether a certain place is unsafe investigate by probing (if possible) and ask yourself the following questions: What is underneath the snow on the ground, and is the snow in such a state that it can cling to the mountain surface (frozen to it or held by blocks, &c.)? Does the snow form a solid mass, or has it distinct layers separated by a soft streak which acts as a lubricant? What is above and below this slope? Does anything threaten from above? Are there supports in the slope or below it? Are there tracks or remains of former avalanches? How were weather and temperature during the last few days, and how are they today? When was the last fall? Is this a snow slab accumulated by wind? &c.

Remember, a safe slope may be rendered dangerous by the presence of a dangerous slope above. Only consider as safe those slopes which are evenly dotted with trees and rocks.

Let me conclude these notes by emphasising once again the need for caution. Under perfect conditions, winter and summer climbing involve much the same risks; but folly and imprudence are much more severely penalised in winter. We are at the beginning of a great development

Christiania to the Left

Christiania in Soft Snow

of winter mountaineering. Skiing, sufficient at least for the purposes of mountaineering, is easy enough to acquire. The problem before us is to transform the ski-runner into a mountaineer, and to tempt mountaineers into the ranks of ski-runners. In summer there is a sound tradition that condemns breaches of the rules of mountaineering. It is our duty to build up a similar tradition in winter. In cricket a bad mistake may lose the match, but unfortunately mountaineering mistakes are more heavily penalised, as the writer has learned to his cost. Only those who have been involved in a mountaineering accident can appreciate the terrible strain of the long, hopeless hours awaiting help.

4

Where to Ski

The Choice of a Good Centre | Alpine Centres |
France | Germany | Austria | Norway | Sweden

The Choice of a Good Centre

The ski-runner in search of a good centre
has several considerations to allow for. He
will naturally have to choose between the
old-established centres and the newer resorts.
Unlike the skater and the tobogganer, he has
as much chance of good sport in the latter as
in the former. Skating rinks and toboggan runs
cannot be built in a season, but skiing slopes
are not dependent on artificial assistance, and
the ski-runner is just as likely to find good
skiing in a new as in an old resort. Nor is it
fair to assume that the best skiing resorts were
the first ones to open. Various considerations
influence the opening of a centre. Well-known

summer resorts stand a very good chance, as they are already well known to the travelling public. They have, moreover, the necessary machinery of hotels and railways. How- ever, it by no means follows that a good summer centre will make a good winter centre. Zermatt is a case in point. Moreover, there are many valleys which afford excellent skiing, but which, owing to difficulties of communication and accommodation, have as yet been unopened.

At the old centres a runner will find more amusements and greater comfort. If he likes to fill his time in with dancing and bridge, he will be better off at one of the old-established favourites, but he will have to pay for these advantages; and if he cares only for the skiing itself, he had far better select a new and comparatively unknown centre. He will pay anything from Fr.10 to Fr.30 for pension per day at any of the better-known centres, and he will find it difficult to get his skiing for less than Fr.7.50 per day anywhere in Switzerland. As regards height, he will do well to bear in mind that a spell of mild weather often visits Central Europe about Christmas-time. If he has to choose his holiday between Christmas-time and the second week in January, he will be unwise to patronise a centre below 4000 feet, and he will do well, if possible, to go above 5000 feet. From the second week in January until the end of February he will be pretty safe between 4000 and 5000 feet, and in good winters excellent skiing may be had between

3000 and 4000 feet. There is also a widespread belief that certain centres enjoy more snow in proportion to their height than others. This claim is made on behalf of Grindelwald and Gstaad, and Grindelwald is certainly cold, partly because it has practically no sunshine and lies in the shadow of a number of high mountains, and possibly because of its nearness to the great glaciers.

A ski-runner, before selecting a centre, should purchase those portions of the Siegfried map which include the surrounding country. He can get these from Björnstad, of Bern, or any other good Swiss firm. The contours on these maps represent a difference in height of 100 feet. If the contours are wide and evenly distributed, and if there are a large number of nicely graded runs facing north or east, he may count on good skiing. If, however, the contours are close together and broken up, and if the map indicates nothing but forests on the easy slopes and no good slopes facing north or east, he may be sure that the skiing will be worthless.

There is much good skiing to be had outside the Alps. The Black Forest is excellent in its way, and the ski-runner who likes to see the best experts at work will find many of them at the Feldberg. Austria is rapidly coming to the fore, and Bohemia is worth a visit. There is much good snow to be found in the Pyrenees, and of course Norway and Sweden oiler endless possibilities. These will be dealt with in the course of the chapter.

Alpine Centres

The following are the chief Alpine skiing centres:

There are a number of well-known resorts in outlying districts of the Alps, such as the Jura. They have certain advantages; they are very cheap and for the most part accessible. You can leave London after lunch and reach Ballaigues early next morning, and it is quite possible to get through from there to London in a day. Thus the ski-runner scores two extra days in his holiday over those who go further inland. The Jura centres suffer from the drawback of low levels. None of their expeditions take the ski-runner above 6000 feet, and in the event of a bad winter he has no higher snow-fields to fall back upon.

The best Jura centres are:

Ballaigues, which is three-quarters of an hour from Vallorbe, the Swiss frontier station. It lies at a height of 3000 feet on the slopes of the Suchet. The Suchet (5235 feet) affords excellent running and, like all these outlying parts of the Jura, has a magnificent view,

Les Ponts (3500 feet) is reached from Vallorbe by a light railway. There are some excellent skiing tours, of which the Dent de Vaulion is perhaps the best.

Mount Soleil (4100 feet), which is reached from St. Imier, is another well-known centre of the Jura with excellent slopes near at hand. For some good ski expeditions in the same

Finish of Christiania to the Right

Halfway Through Christiania to the Left

category as the Jura centres we may mention Rigi, where the Rigi Kaltbad Hotel has been recently opened (4805 ft.). All these centres are excellent in a normal winter, but suffer severely in such an abnormally bad season as the last.

There are a number of well-known resorts above the Lake of Geneva, such as Caux (3610 feet), which is reached by funicular from Territet, and Les Avants (3260 feet). They are rather too low and sunny to give good skiing and are more famous as bobsleighing and tobogganing centres. Château d'Oex (3203 feet) is rather better, but suffers severely in a bad winter. There are a number of good centres on the Montreux-Oberland line. In a good winter Gstaad is as fine a skiing centre as a man could want. Its height is 3897 feet. There are a variety of excellent tours, such as the Windspillen, Wasserngrat, Mattenberg, and Hornberg (The *A.S.C. Guide to the Bernese Oberland, Part I*, gives full particulars of the skiing expeditions in the region of the Oberland west of the Gemmi. It can be obtained from Mr Horace Marshall and Son for 2*s*. 2*d*. post free). Other stations on the Montreux-Oberland line which afford excellent skiing are Saanen (3350 feet) and Zweisimmen (3267 feet).

There are many well-known centres branching off from the Rhone Valley. Villars-sur-Ollon (4120 feet) is reached by an electric railway from Bex in forty-five minutes. The most famous skiing tour is the Chamossaire (6940 feet), but in the height of the season this run is too popular to afford good snow, and a better run is the Chaux Ronde de Taveyannaz (6644 feet) and the Bovonnaz Alp (6400 feet). There are a number of fine skiing passes. Adelboden can bo reached in two days via Lauenen and Lenk. The passes to Adelboden are none of them higher than 7000 feet and afford excellent running. They are best taken from Villars to Adelboden (for other expeditions see *A.S.C. Guide*). Diablerets (3816 ft.) is easily reached from Villars over the Col de la Croix, or from Aigle by carriage or sleigh. There are some good skiing expeditions in the district. Facing Villars in valleys which branch off from the Rhone Valley to the west, lie Champéry (3450 feet) and Morgins (4510 feet). Champéry affords fair and Morgins excellent skiing. Morgins is, indeed, one of the best skiing centres in Switzerland, though the fact has not yet been recognised. There are some excellent runs from Morgins, such as the Pas de Soleil, the Bellevue and Corbeaux, and there are many good skiing passes to Champéry and Sixt. Leysin and Le Sepey, which can be reached from Aigle, are well spoken of.

The Rhone Valley takes a sharp bend at Martigny. A few stations higher lies Sierre, from which Montana (5005 feet) is reached by railway. Montana is famous for its sun and for its panorama, and there is good skiing to be had in the district. The Zaat (7293 feet) is a favourite short tour. Cri Ders (8251 feet) and Zabona (8297 feet) are easily reached by following the ridge. The Col de Pochet (8169 feet) is an excellent expedition. The Col de Bonvin (7890 feet) also gives good running. A favourite long tour is the Plaine Morte Glacier and Wildstrubel Hut (9115 feet). An excellent little inn has been opened near the Wildstrubel Hut, and the guardian will come up from Lenk if required by telegram or telephone. The Wildstrubel is climbed from this, the Rohrbachhaus, and it is easy to reach Kandersteg over the Wildstrubel, or Lenk over the Wildhorn. Though Montana faces south, many of these runs are on eastern slopes and afford excellent snow throughout the season.

Letjkerbad (4660 feet) is another popular winter centre that can be reached from the Rhone Valley, and the favourite skiing tours fire the Torrenthorn, Wildstrubel, and Gitzifurka.

In the Oberland there are numberless centres. Lenk can be reached from Zweisimmen, and has just been opened. Its height is 3267 feet, and in a good season the skiing from Lenk is as good as you can wish.

Adelboden (4500 feet) is reached via Spiez and Frutigen. The railway goes as far as Frutigen, thence by sleigh for two or three hours. Adelboden is one of the oldest and most famous of winter centres, and there are few better places for a beginner. There are a variety of excellent runs of all grades of difficulty, but they have one common disadvantage. Very few of them bring one back to the hotel; a walk of forty-five minutes on the level is the almost invariable prelude and conclusion to a day's running.

The Schwandfehlspitz (6650 feet) is a small and easy tour, and the same can be said of the Kuenisbergli (5710 feet). Long tours which give excellent skiing are the Halienmoos (6410 feet), Laveigrat (7395 feet), Elighorn (7695 feet), and Bonderspitz (8360 feet). The Wildstrubel is more easily climbed from Kandersteg, and the direct ascent from Adelboden is dangerous. There are excellent skiing passes to the Grimmi and Lenk, and a very favourite combination tour is to cross to Lenk in the morning, ascending to the Wildhorn Hut; on the second day cross the Wildhorn to the WildstrubelHut, finishing by the traverse of the Wildstrubel to Kandersteg, and thence to Adelboden by sleigh. Montana can, of course, be reached over the Wildstrubel, and Villars can be reached in two days via Lenk, Gsteig, and Diablerets. For other long tours see the *A.S.C. Guide*.

Grimmi Alp (4133 feet), which was opened last season, is assured of a great future as a skiing centre. There are plenty of excellent north slopes, and several of the runs lead back straight to the hotel. The Grimmi Pass is a favourite tour and gives excellent skiing for about 3000 ft. Another good expedition is to Ottemgrat Pass, between the Gsür and Männlifluh, while the Abendberg is a favourite run, especially with local clubs.

Kandersteg (3900 feet) is a good centre for serious mountaineering on ski, but there is a lack of small expeditions. The snow, however, is usually in good condition. The favourite tours are the Wildstrubel and the Tschingel Pass. The Bonderkrinden is an excellent skiing pass leading over to Adelboden, and the passes to Mürren and to the Kienthal are also of very high quality (see also, *A.S.C. Guide*).

Beatenberg (3800 feet) lies on the slopes above Thun. It is very sunny, rather too sunny for the ski-runner, but there is some pleasant running to be found on the slopes of the Amisbühl and the Niederhorn.

Mürren (5387 feet). This is one of the most famous skiing centres, and owing to its height, it suffers less than any other centre in the Oberland from warm weather. The favourite shor tour is to cross three low passes to the railway station of Grütsch and to take the train home. The Wasenegg gives about 2000 ft. of first-class skiing. The Schilthorn (9754 feet) is a longer expedition; it is not difficult and gives some very varied running. The Sefinen Furgge, the Büttlassen (10,490 feet), and the Tschingel Pass (9270 feet) are among the longer expeditions that can be done from this centre. There is much good ground for ski-runners to be explored in the Sausthal, which can be reached from the Bietenlücke.

Wengen (4180 feet). Wengen has the advantage of a sports train which carries ski-runners up to a height of nearly 6000 ft. The favourite expedition is to take this train, then climb for half an hour to the Scheidegg Pass and run down to Grindehvald. The Eiger Tunnel and the snow slopes leading up the base of the Eiger Rocks also afford good skiing ground. Wengen is now connected with the Jungfrau-Joch by the new Jungfrau Railway, which carries the ski-runner to the height of 11,000 ft. This line will be open in winter, and ski-runners will be able to leave Wengen at three o'clock in the morning, reaching the Jungfrau-Joch at about seven o'clock, and thence ski down the Aletsch Glacier, across the Lötschenlücke to the Lötschenthal, and return to Wengen the same night by the new Lötschberg Tunnel. Grindelwald (3450 feet). This is one of the oldest established of Swiss centres. It is rather low, but, owing to the fact that it gets very little sun and is in the shade most of the day, it has as much snow as places of a higher altitude, and in a cold winter skiing from Grindelwald is as good as, if not better than, from any other place in the Alps. There is excellent running to be had on the two Scheideggs, Faulhorn, Schwarzhorn, Männlichen, &c., and the Jungfrau Railway makes the exploration of the upper glaciers extremely easy.

Other centres in the outlying part of the Oberland are Andermatt (4817 feet) and Engelberg (3412 feet). There is splendid skiing to be had from both these centres. The Titlis is the favourite long tour from Engelberg.

The Grisons contain some of the best skiing in the Alps.

Davos (5250 feet) is probably the best all-round skiing centre in Switzerland. The Bremendbühl (7348 feet) is a short three hours' climb. The Jacobshorn (8430 feet) is somewhat longer, and the Kublistour is perhaps the very finest day tour in Switzerland. The Parsen Eurka (7920 feet) is reached from Wolfgang

(5308 feet) in two or three hours. From these there is continuous and excellent skiing down to Kublis (2680 feet). All these tours afford good skiing, and there are many others, of which the Schwarzhorn (10,240 feet) is one of the more popular long ones. There is a good local ski club at Davos, and there are few places where the ski-runner has more opportunities of practising his sport.

Lenzerheide (4770 feet). After Davos, Lenzerheide is perhaps the best skiing centre in Switzerland. Before it was opened to English visitors it was selected for two courses held by Norwegian skiers in the early days of skiing. There is a wide choice of full-day tours and excellent practice slopes. The Stätzerhorn (8460 feet) and the other heights in the region all give first-class ski-running. There are also good passes to Arosa and Davos.

Arosa (6000 feet) is chiefly famous for tobogganing, but, like most of the Grisons centres, skiing is very varied and uniformly excellent. The best runs are the Weisshorn (8720 feet) and Rothorn (9780 feet). There is a good skiing pass to Davos.

Upper Engadine. St. Moritz (6190 feet). Owing to its great height, St. Moritz is an excellent place in a bad winter, but the skiing from it is not of a very high quality. There is some very good mountaineering on ski to be found in the Bernina group, but the short tours are not so good as at Davos. There is, however, a very pleasant run on the Muottas Murail, and before the snow gets crusted the southern slopes of the Pitz Nain (10,045 feet) afford good running. The Corvatsch is a long tour and is said to be excellent.

Campfer (6020 feet) lies three miles from St. Moritz and is slightly nearer the best skiing, and, like St. Moritz, is a good place in a warm winter.

Pontresina (6000 feet) is a very popular centre with German visitors. There are some good practice slopes near the village, but there is no really good short run ending up at Pontresina. By using sleighs and trains, one can get some very good skiing in the district, and, owing to its height and the near presence of glaciers, it is a good place in warm weather. There is, of course, some fine mountaineering to be done in the Bernina group.

Celerina (5740 feet) and Samaden (5670 feet) are centres which are becoming very popular. They are both stations on the railway line to St. Moritz, and Samaden especially has some very fine skiing.

France

There is some excellent skiing in the French Alps. Chamounix (3415 feet) is, of course, the most famous winter resort. There is some good running on the slopes of the Col de Balme and the Col do Voza, and those who go in for more serious work will find the Col de Chardonnet a fine pass. The Col de Géant has also been crossed on ski, but is far better taken from Courmayeur than from Chamounix. Mont Blanc is occasionally climbed.

The snow is even better at Argentières (4100 feet); this is about five miles from Chamounix.

In the Dauphiné, St. Pierre de Chartreuse (3785 feet) and the Villard de Lans (3415 feet) are said to have good skiing.

Cauterets, in the High Pyrenees, and various centres in the Maritime Alps are also visited by enterprising ski-runners.

Germany

There are a number of skiing centres in Germany, such as Garmisch (2300 feet) and Kohlgrub (2700 feet), but the ski-runner who has Alpine, Swiss, Norwegian, and Austrian centres to choose from will hardly be tempted by these centres, which are chiefly of value to Germans living in the neighbourhood. The Feldberg (4900 feet) is another matter, and all ski-runners should spend at least a week at this famous centre. They will see the best experts at work, and will come away with greatly extended ideas of the possibilities of the sport.

The skiing in the Black Forest is of a different type from Alpine work, and consists, for the most part, of long days across low-lying hills; the snow is usually excellent. A characteristic of all Black Forest skiing is the extent of open wood, which affords first-class running. Other well-known Black Forest centres are Titisee (2816 feet) and Schönwald (3000 feet).

Austria

Austria is rapidly coming to the fore as a skiing country. The travelling facilities are excellent and the communication between centres is much easier than in the Alps. The most famous centres are Cortina (4026 feet) and St. Anton (4270 feet), both of which are in the Vorarlberg and Tirol. Cortina has excellent practice slopes and good half-day excursions. It is, however, not such a good centre for long full-day climbs as St. Anton. Kitzbühel (2600 feet) is also a very popular skiing centre.

In Styria, Mittendorf (2600 feet) and Aussee (2135 feet) seem to be the most popular centres.

In Lower Austria, Lilienfeld has been rendered famous—one might almost say notorious—as the home of Zdarsky. There are many centres in Bohemia and Carinthia which are becoming popular, and the ski-runner who likes exploring fresh ground and to spend his time crossing from valley to valley might do worse than spend a few weeks in Bohemia and Carinthia.

Montenegro is sure to afford good skiing, and pioneer work has still to be done in Albania.

Track of a Christiania

Norway

No ski-runner's education is complete without a visit to Norway, and, fortunately, the skiing in Norway is ideal just when the snow is deteriorating in Switzerland. No ski-runner should visit Norway before Easter, as only the limited district of Nordmarken, near Christiania, is of any use for skiing before the beginning of March. In the mountain districts the early winter is a succession of storms.

Travelling in Norway is comparatively cheap, and the cost per day of a trip to Norway should work out at a rather lower amount than at the average Swiss centre. Unfortunately, the main districts are not easy to get at and accommodation is difficult. There are no club huts in the Jotunheimen, and at Easter-time Bessheim and similar places are apt to be rather crowded.

Skiing in Norway is very different from skiing in the Alps. The slopes are gentler and the risk of avalanches is almost negligible.

None of the mountains are higher than 9000 feet, and Norwegian skiing rarely involves an ascent of more than three or four thousand feet at a time. The great difficulty is the lack of accommodation, and the enterprising runner is often forced to try a form of skiing which is very rarely practised in the Alps. He can go for weeks, dragging his sleeping-bag on a sleigh and leaving it to make occasional ascents in the neighbourhood of his camp. He will have to sleep for night3 together with no protection but the sleeping-bag, and this form of skiing will be found very different from that which is practised in Switzerland, where the runner returns night after night to a comfortable hotel. It has, however, its own charm and its own difficulties. The following are the chief centres:

The ski-runner will probably begin at Christiania, where he cannot do better than put up for a day or two at Voksenkollen. The skiing possibilities of Christiania are described on pp.198-199. The principal skiing districts are as follows:

The Dovre Mountains district, in which the best centre is Röros (2065 feet).

Jotunheim. There are a number of centres in the Jotunheim, of which Bessheim (3100 feet) is the most popular. The winter terms are Kr.5.00 a day, all included (Kr.18.00 = £1). The hotel is of wood and is clean and good, and the food is excellent of its kind.

Bessheim. For much excellent information on Norwegian skiing, I refer the reader to Mr J.H.W. Fulton's book With *Ski in Norway and Lapland* and also to his article in the current number of the *Alpine Ski Club Annual*. Bessheim is a splendid skiing country, and the following are the one-day expeditions: Besshö (7590 feet), about eight hours. The route is via the east end of Bessvand (or crosswise by the Bessvand Hills, which skirt the north shore of the lake) to the Besshö Glacier. The glacier should be crossed on the left side of the precipitous rocks leading up to the summit, and the ridge should be followed to the top. The expedition is quite safe and easy, and affords wonderful running. Nautgarstind (7600 feet) is also an eight hours' climb which gives good running. Other expeditions are the Heimdalshö (6000 feet) and the Sikkilsdalshö (6000 feet). Another good centre is Glitterheim, which is reached from Randsvaerk, Hindsaeter, or Bessheim—

the latter way only by ski, as no sleigh road exists between Glitterheim and Bessheim. The hotel is not usually open before Easter, but can be opened specially if application is made to Herr Tronheims, of Randsvaerk. From here the Glittertind can be climbed on ski.

Fefor Sanatorium is described on p.200, Other centres in Norway are Storfjeldsaeter Sanatorium, in the Rondane Mountains; Bolkesjö Hotel, in the Telemark district; and Fjeldsaeter Sanatorium, in the Trondjhem district.

There are also a few excellent skiing centres on the Christiania-Bergen line; of these Finse is the most important, and it is fully described further on..

Lapland. There are some excellent skiing centres in Lapland which are very little known to English runners. Mr Fulton was, I believe, the first English runner to explore them.

Abisko, Sweden-Lapland Railway; between Riksgränsen and Kiruna. Excellent skiing amongst mountains there, none of which are more than about 1500 to 2000 feet above sea level, and situated on the shore of the huge Lake Torne Trask.

Riksgränsen (frontier). There is quite good skiing in the neighbourhood.

Kiruna (1600 feet) is an interesting place, but mostly flat country; some hills, such as Luossavare and Adriamvare. There is an excellent hotel called the Ternvags Hotellet, which is very clean and comfortable, and the terms are about Kr.8.5 per day.

Gellivare, about 1100 feet and a little over two hours by train from Kiruna. The hotel is very fair. There is some good skiing on Gollivaro Dundret (2700 feet), otherwise the country is flat. Elk may be found, but not shot; the surrounding district is fir country, but birch country prevails round Kiruna.

Kebnekaise and adjacent Lapland Mountains in winter. The former is upwards of fifty miles from Kiruna, which is the nearest civilisation, though there are a few scattered Finn villages to within twenty-five miles of the mountains.

There is a good stone hut called Kebne kaisestugan, from which Kebnekaise may be climbed. This hut is used in summer by tourists; perhaps thirty people in all. The key may be obtained from Herr Fors, Kiruna.

Many of the mountains most easily accessible from the hut are not well suited for skiing, having rather steep sides and more or less flat tops, but the following would be good:

Skartatjåkko, to the south; Tarfallatjåkko, a long distance to the north; Tjauratjåkko, to the east. There is probably excellent skiing on Kebnekaise Glacier from rocks of the mountain itself in an easterly direction to the end of the glacier and out by the Tarfalladalen to the Ladtjovagge, in which is the hut. One arm of this glacier and the' Kaskassa Glacier, which comes down from the north between the Kaskassatjåkko and the Tarfallatjåkko, both calve into a lake, at the foot of the Kaskassatjåkko. The Savopahkte (also to the south) would probably afford some fair running.

Good skiing can be obtained from Tromsö on the mainland, and also on some of the islands; also from Harstad. Good skiing can also be obtained behind the great Svartisen Glacier, which runs parallel with the coast between Sandnessjöen and Bödö, *i.e.* a three or four days' expedition from Saltdalen to Mö, sleeping in the huts built to shelter workmen looking after the telegraph wires.

Either Saltdalen or Mö might be stayed at for skiing purposes. From the former the Sulitelma can be ascended and an expedition made to Beieren. From Mö the Svartisen Glacier can be reached. (See pp. 246-248 in *With Ski in Norway and Lapland*.)

Another interesting trip by ski and reindeer-sleigh can be made from Bosseköp, in the far north (Alten Fjord), across Lapland to Kiruna or Gellivare. Lapps and sleighs (reindeer) are necessary, also sleeping-bags and food, though—bar- ring accidents—one would not have to sleep in the open. The route is via Kantokeino and Karesuando. Passports are necessary, as an arm of Finland is crossed. The expedition can be fitted out from Hammerfest. Or from Bosseköp to Karasjok, and so to Vardö or Vadsö.

Sweden

The best winter sports centre in Sweden is Are (about 1400 feet). Are is about seventeen hours' train journey from Stockholm and seventeen hours' journey from Trondjhem. There are some excellent hotels, especially the Grand Hotel, where the terms are Kr.6-7 a day inclusive ; evening dress advisable. There is some very good skiing in the district.

Another good centre is Storlien, which is on the railway between Are and Trondjhem. This is the frontier station. Högfjails Pensionsttet is also comfortable and moderate. Hindäss (450 feet) is twenty-two miles, and less even than an hour in a train from Gothenburg. Stockholm, the capital, is, of course, well worth a visit.

5

Skiing Through the High Alps

*The Bernese Oberland and its Traverses |
East and West Wing of the Oberland | High-
Level Route to Zermatt | Skiing from Saas-Fee
| The Bernina Group | The Ortler and Gross
Glockner*

In the last chapter I have tried to give a brief
outline of the more famous skiing centres in
Europe. The mountaineer, however, is not
dependent on any particular centres. Wherever
he can find a small inn and a club hut he can
climb, and as there is scarcely any Alpine valley
in which he cannot find accommodation for
the night, he has a vide choice of routes.

There is still much new country to be
explored on ski, but thanks to the good work
of Continental runners our knowledge of the
high Alps in winter is rapidly increasing. I
advise the winter mountaineer to get hold of the
back numbers of the *Alpine Ski Club Annual*

of which the fifth number is now in the press, the three numbers of the *Mitteleuropaischen Ski-Verbandes* that have appeared up to date, and the first seven numbers of *Ski* the year-book of the Swiss Ski Association.

The Bernese Oberland and its Traverses

The Bernese Oberland is in my opinion the finest of all fields for high Alp skiing. The glaciers are greater than in other parts of the Alps, and such good judges as Sir Martin Conway assert that, 'the great snow highway from Ried in the Lötschenthal to Meiringen is the finest thing of its kind in the Alps'. This traverse is described on pp.231-241 of this book. The Aletsch glacier is now rendered very accessible to ski-runners by the Jungfrau line, which will run in summer and winter to the Jungfrau-Joch, which is more than 11,000 feet. above the sea. A number of peaks have been climbed by ski-runners in this district, and amongst others the Finsteraarhorn, Aletschhorn, Fiescherhorn, Monch, and Jungfrau. The reader is referred to the second, third, and fifth numbers of the *Alpine Ski Club Annual* and to the seventh number of the *S.C.G.B. Year-book* in which a well-known Swiss ski-runner, Herr Motte, describes an ascent of the Fiescherhorn.

This, the Ried-Meiringen route, is the finest traverse in the Oberland, but there are numbers of other skiing passes worthy of notice. The

How Not to Jump

How to Jump

Tschingel pass from Mürren to Kandersteg was one of the first to be crossed on ski, and is still a favourite. The Tschingelhorn is often climbed from the Mutthorn hut on the summit of the Tschingel, and last winter with Edward Tennant I climbed the Lauterbrunnen Breithorn. A very pleasant variation of the Tschingel is to branch off down the Gamchi-lücke instead of descending to Lauterbrunnen. The Gamchi-lücke is an ideal skiing pass. The scenery is of a very high order, and the running is far superior to any enjoyed on the Tschingel. The Gamchi-lücke leads down to the Kienthal, which has so far not been opened up in winter. It should prove an excellent centre for ambitious mountaineers. The Blumlisalp and Gspaltenhorn have already been climbed. The reader must understand throughout that I am referring to winter climbing, and that the omission of any actual reference to skiing or winter climbing is intended to avoid needless repetition

Grindelwald, of course, is a centre for some excellent work. The Aletsch snowfield is easily, reached by means of the Jungfrau Railway, and the Wetterhorn, Schreckhorn, and Eiger have been climbed on many occasions. None of these are skiing trips, though ski can be used up to a certain point on the Schreckhorn and Eiger. Ski are useless for the ascent of the Wetterhorn from rindelwald, but this mountain gives some excellent running if taken from the Urbach-Thal.

The two wings of the Oberland are favourite hunting-grounds with the ski-runner. The western wing includes the Wildstrubel, Wildhorn, and

Diablerets. None of these summits touch 11,000 feet, but they are all glacier-capped, and were among the first snow mountains to be climbed on ski. They present no difficulty, and are an excellent introduction to more serious work. Professor Roget was the first to carry out a very fine high- level route across the three summits. He left Gsteig and ascended to the Diablerets hut on the first day, crossed both the Diablerets and Wildhorn on the second day, and on the third crossed the Wildstrubel to Kandersteg. The running throughout was excellent.

East and West Wing of the Oberland

The eastern wing of the Oberland includes the range whose snows give birth to the Rhone glacier. There is some very fine skiing in this district, and among other peaks the Galenstock seems to be a favourite. The seventh issue of *Ski* the organ of the Swiss Ski Association, contains an account of some summer skiing in this part of the world. Further east still there is the Titlis group. The Titlis shares with the Wildstrubel the distinction of being the most favourite introduction to skiing in the high Alps. The valleys round the Todi are not well known to ski-runners, and I have never heard of anybody taking ski to the summit of the Todi. That it has been climbed by ski-runners is, however, almost a certainty, but the ski-runner in search of novelty should be able to find new ground in this district.

So much for the Oberland and its outlying groups. As this chapter is chiefly concerned with long traverses and not so much with climbs from a centre I will now pass on to describe another famous high-level route. It is a matter of opinion, but I fancy that the big Oberland traverse is as fine as anything in the Alps. It has a serious rival in the high-level route from Chamounix to Zermatt. Those familiar with Alpine literature will remember that this route was a favourite with early explorers, and the gradual linking-up of the connecting passes forms a very romantic story. The first attempt to cross the Pennine Alps on ski from west to east was made by four Chamounix climbers, Dr Payot, Joseph Couttet, Alfred Simond, and the guide Joseph Ravanel, nicknamed 'Le Rouge'. They were prevented by bad weather from carrying out then- plan, but nevertheless they crossed much new ground. They were forced to retreat on the Col de l'Evêque, and to descend via the Val de Bagnes to Martigny. Thence they made for Evolena and crossed the Col d'Hérens to Zermatt. This sporting expedition took place in 1903, and is fully described in the *Revue Alpine* for that year.

High-Level Route to Zermatt

There were various other attempts before the route was finally proved to be skiable by Professor Roget. Professor Roget did not start from Chamounix, as the high level proper begins at Bourg St. Pierre, on the route to the Grand St. Bernard. If you begin the tour from Chamounix you must drop down into the valleys, and the high-level route, properly so called, begins at Bourg St. Pierre and ends at Zermatt.

From Bourg St. Pierre this party travelled along an almost unbroken ice route to Zermatt. Chanrion, which is about 8000 feet above the sea-level, is the only point in this route which is not entirely surrounded by ice.

The party consisted of Professor Roget and another famous Swiss mountaineer, Marcel Kurz. They engaged four guides, Maurice and Jules Crettex, Louis Theytaz of Zinal, Leonce Murisier of Praz de Fort. On January 9, 1911, they left Bourg St. Pierre and climbed to the Valsorey hut. On the second day they crossed the Gol du Sonadon to the Chanrion hut. On the third day they crossed in succession the Col de l'Evêque, Col de Colon, and the Col de Bertol. They passed the night in the Bertol hut, climbed the Dent Blanche on the next day, and on the fifth day from the start crossed from the Bertol hut to Zermatt by the Col d'Hérens. This is one of the finest expeditions that have been carried out in the winter Alps.

This party was soon-followed by Dr Koenig of Geneva, who followed much the same route, but climbed the Combin instead of the Dent Blanche. The Combin had been previously climbed by Professor Roget from the Panossiere hut, and a description of the ascent is contained in the first number of the *Alpine Ski Club Annual*. The high-level route to Zermatt is described by Professor Roget in the third number. It would, of course, be possible to vary this route by climbing any of the mountains that rise from its passes. The Ruinette, Mont Blanc de Seilon, Mont Collon, and Pigne d'Arolla are tempting propositions. Shortly after Professor Roget's successful expedition one of the guides who had accompanied it tried to repeat part of the route with Mr Moore of the Alpine Ski Club.

Ski are also of some use for the ascent of the Zinal Rothorn, Gabelhorn, and Weishorn, but these mountains will attract only the genuine winter mountaineer, for whom ski are merely a means to an end. The Dom and Täschhorn belong to the same category.

Skiing from Saas-Fee

Saas-Fee, like Zermatt, is not open in winter, and like Zermatt it is a splendid centre for winter mountaineering. I refer the reader to the seventh issue of *Ski* for an article by Herr Supersaxo, in which he describes ski ascents of the Joderhorn, Portjenpass, and Allalinhorn.

The Bernina Group

The Oberland and the Pennines will give the mountaineer as much good work as he is likely to want for many seasons. When he wearies of these ranges he should try the Bernina group. Here there is a splendid field for glacier traverses. Perhaps the finest full day's skiing on record was accomplished in this district by Marcel Kurz. He and a friend left the Bernina hospice at 6.30, and worked their way across the Palii glacier. Twilight found them ascending the last slopes of the Fuorcla Sella. They ran down the Roseg glacier the same night to Pontresina. Anybody who follows this terrific run on the map will realise the energy required to carry it through in one day, *A.S.C. Annual, No. 4.*

The Palü and Bernina and other summits of this chain have been climbed in winter, but are not very tempting to the ski-runner.

There are some excellent passes further south. A fine route leads from Sils up the Vais Fex and across glacier passes either to Pontresina or the Bernina hospice. Still further south we find the Forno group and the Forno glacier, both of which have been explored in winter. That plucky lady climber, Mrs Le Blond, has climbed the Disgrazzia in winter, and though the distance to be covered is very great, I fancy the ski-runner might find some good work in this wing of the Bernina group.

The Ortler and Gross Glockner

The eastern wing of the Alps has its own problems. The Ortler and Gross Glockner have been climbed by ski-runners, and further east still Tirol offers some fascinating ground. But, to my mind, there are no traverses in the whole range of the Alps from the Maritimes to Carinthia to compare with the high-level routes across the Pennines and Oberland. Industrious explorers of the Dauphiny and the Graians may prove this statement to be unduly optimistic, but I fancy it will stand unchallenged for many a day.

6

Clubs, Competitions and Tests

Skiing Clubs and Their History | Competition and the Style Element | Skiing Tests

Skiing Clubs and Their History

The beginner will probably find it worth his while to join some sort of a skiing club. The inside history of the various skiing clubs is in its way quite entertaining. In 1903 Richardson and a few other enthusiastic ski-runners founded the Ski Club of Great Britain. The club started with a low subscription, five shillings, and no entrance qualification. Ladies were freely admitted. As so often happens when a club is started by friends, the original constitution was very lax and the rules liable to many interpretations; and, as equally often happens, the club passed out of the control of its original founders. A new committee came into power who pursued a policy utterly alien from the intentions of the original members, greatly, I think, to the club's harm. Richardson, who financed the club from the start, was treated with scant courtesy, and his various schemes for enlarging the club on a broad and comprehensive basis were defeated. The change of policy was occasioned by the birth of a new club. In 1908 the Alpine Ski Club was founded for winter mountaineers. The original founders felt that the Ski Club of Great Britain catered for those who were primarily interested in skiing as a sport in itself. We left tests and competitions to the older club. We admitted a certain number of original members without qualifications, but since then we have raised the standard every year. We have published an annual which contains accounts of the best climbing done in the winter Alps, and I think we may fairly claim to represent the British winter mountaineers, just as the older club represented those for whom the sport of skiing was an end in itself.

Now if the S.C.G.B. had proceeded on its original lines it would undoubtedly have had a membership of two thousand to-day instead of a paltry three hundred. But the Alpine Ski Club frightened them. A prominent member of the committee dashed round to see Mr Richardson and remarked that the A.S.C., modelled as it was on the Alpine Club, would undoubtedly become the crack skiing club. He added that the S.C.G.B. must strive to imitate the A.S.C.

This they did pretty thoroughly. They raised their subscription to one guinea ; they copied our proposal form; they imitated our entrance qualification. They, further, approached us with a view to amalgamation, and we declined on the ground that they had lady members. The committee decided to deprive the ladies of their privileges. They canvassed vigorously, and carried their motion by a majority of one. The next year was spent in taking counsel's opinion, and Richardson, who put up a gallant fight for the ladies, forced the committee to withdraw their original proposals.

A sensitive committee would have resigned after their policy had received such an unequivocal vote of censure. But the committee of the S.C.G.B. took their beating philosophically, and proceeded to interpret the rules so as to encourage the government of permanent officials beyond the reach of an adverse ballot. The committee do not come up for election as a whole. Three members retire every year, but at the last general meeting two of these were the president and secretary, who promptly became *ex officio* members. One vacancy was thrown open to election, and the fortunate candidate had things made so unpleasant for him that he resigned. The only member of the original committee who resigned returned as a representative of an affiliated club.

A party, of whom the present writer was a humble supporter, decided that nothing could be hoped from a club whose constitution made the committee all-powerful and secure against any change of sentiment. Moreover, we wished to return to the policy of those who founded the club.

The subscription of the S.C.G.B. is a guinea, and their entrance qualification is a compromise. A candidate who has done thirty days' skiing is considered eligible. This qualification is too low to give the club prestige as an exclusive body, and too high to make it representative of the rank-and-file.

The British Ski Association was therefore founded to meet the needs of the situation. Like the older body, it is a members' club, controlled entirely by its members. Unlike the older club, its committee is also controlled by the members. It provides tests and competitions for its members, publishes a review twice a year, and provides a central storing-house where ski may be warehoused and stored free of charge. The subscription is 5s.

The B.S.A. made various proposals to the S.C.G.B. in order to avoid a breach. These were declined. The committee of the S.C.G.B. showed once more a sincere form of flattery. Just as they had imitated the A.S.C., so now they proceeded to imitate the B.S.A. They founded a body on similar lines, a belated recognition of the wishes of the club. Where the B.S.A. offered to warehouse ski and oil them for nothing, they proposed to store, not oil, but ski and ski-gear (a nasty knock; we had forgotten ski-gear). Next week we shall hear of a club that will oil (but not store) ski and stretch Laupaars.

Unfortunately for the founders of the N.S.U. they had forgotten to consult the club before launching this new body on the world. Various members of the club, including two ex-presidents, complained bitterly of their unconstitutional conduct in the columns of the Field. All the best opinion was in favour of striking up a compromise and amalgamating the three bodies. A special general meeting was summoned, and the committee only escaped by seven votes a censure for founding the N.S.U. without consulting the club. A member moved that the committee come up for election every year, as they do in all good sporting clubs. This motion was not opposed by a single speech. The committee hastily put it to the vote, and their supporters obediently defeated it again by a narrow majority. Finally, Mr Richardson moved that the meeting appoint two members to reopen negotiations with the B.S.A. with a view to peace, and here again the committee proved intractable. Every sensible ski-runner must regret the situation.

The situation is, roughly, this: A club can either be select and preserve a high standard of admission, like the Alpine Club, or it can be representative and powerful and all-embracing like the Swiss Alpine Club. In the first case the members will cheerfully pay a high subscription for the prestige of membership; in the latter they may reasonably expect good value for their money. This, of course, the Swiss Alpine Club gives, as two journeys to Zermatt save the subscription, owing to the reduced rates allowed to the club. Let us apply this test to the skiing clubs. A member of the Alpine Ski Club pays half a guinea a year for an annual which would otherwise cost him 2*s*, and the right to go to the formal and informal dinners of the club. He may also feel a justifiable pleasure in wearing the badge of the club, for it represents a certain standard of experience in winter mountaineering. A member of the British Ski Association gets 2*s'* worth of literature and various privileges for 5*s*. If he leaves his ski at the warehouse he saves his subscription and has the reviews thrown in. In time we may get concessions from the railways, and even now I fancy members will get good value for their money. The S.C.G.B., on the other hand, charges a guinea for a 2*s* year-book and the right to attend certain dinners. No one can pretend that the prestige of having done thirty days' skiing is worth the remaining 16*s*.

I think it is easy to attach too much importance to clubs. A club is originally started to promote some sport or other. Sooner or later the enthusiastic members care a good deal more about the club than the sport, and if a rival club admittedly did more for the sport they would none the less pray for its sudden death. Personally I am far keener on the sport than the club, and if the club fails to promote the sport in the best manner open to it no sense of loyalty would prevent me aiding a more efficient body. After all, the chief object of a skiing club is to amuse us during the weary summer months when skiing is a memory. One should not take them too seriously. They are not, as some suppose, a matter of life and death, and British runners will continue to exist even if the A.S.C., the S.C.G.B., and the B.S.A. wind up tomorrow. I am always sorry when men show a tendency to turn a disagreement about policy into a personal feud. I have, I hope, many friends on the committee of the S.C.G.B., though I disagree with their views on club matters. And, fortunately, we forget these secondary issues when once the snow begins to whiten the hills. And when next we find ourselves three thousand feet above the valley with six good inches of powder- snow beneath our feet, not one of us would barter the next half-hour for the supremacy of this or that body of ski-runners.

Competitions and the Style Element

The question of clubs brings one naturally to the problem of competitions. I have seen at various times many skiing races, and from a somewhat varied experience I have learned that the finest and most conclusive test of skiing is a downhill race without sticks. I think most people will agree that the element of personal bias should be reduced to a minimum. The stop-watch has no pet theories on style, the tape-measure has no views on the proper position of the jumper while in the air. Once let in this mysterious factor, style, and the competition is certain to be judged on subjective prejudices. In Norway the situation is still further complicated by the fact that their big competitions are decided on the combined results of a race and a jump. The jump, moreover, is decided partly by length and partly by style. You will have some sympathy with the difficulties of the judges when you try to determine what mark A shall have, who wins the jump by two metres in fair style and comes in second in the long distance by two minutes. Who shall decide between him and B, who wins the long distance, and, though beaten in the jump by two metres, jumps in perfect style? Surely any decision based on such unrelated data must be largely a matter of individual caprice. Style in skiing, unlike style in skating, does not conform to any objective standard. That style is best, both in jumping and racing, which produces the best results. The man who jumps in the best style will usually jump farthest; a bad stylist may sometimes fluke a long jump, but such accidents are inseparable from the nature of all competitions, and it is far better to risk the prize falling once in ten times to an inferior performer than to challenge the accusation of partiality or bad judging from the supporters of the beaten candidate. You can't dispute the tape-measure, but you can have very lively arguments on the subject of style. In Switzerland jumps are marked solely on length the better method, as it seems to me.

The arguments I have advanced against marking style apply with even more force against competitions in which jumping and racing are marked together. Each is a distinct branch of the art. But long-distance racing has its own problems oven when you have decided not to mark the runners on style. In the old days of racing the competitors usually had as much climbing as downhill running. The best man often won, but on many occasions the race went to a man who was merely a strong climber. Sometimes it was won by a competitor whose ski were rough, and who was thus enabled to take a very direct uphill course. The difference between a good and average performer uphill works out at about ten minutes in a thousand feet, whereas the difference between a good and an average performer for the same distance downhill works out at about three minutes. So that a good hill-climber who was only average downhill would beat a good downhill runner who was not a very strong climber by seven minutes. This is obviously absurd, for though uphill skiing is an important branch of the art, no one could pretend that it demands the skill and balance essential to down- hill running. Nerve and dash obviously are negligible factors in the ascent. Further, no sensible man would dream of dashing uphill on ski save in a race, whereas every decent ski- runner wants to go downhill as quickly as possible.

So that uphill racing bears no relation to practice, whereas a race downhill is on the natural lines of all good skiing.

Ruling uphill racing out of the question, we have still an important point to consider. Shall candidates be allowed sticks? I think there are good reasons for prohibiting the use of sticks. A really steady stick-rider will beat all but the most brilliant stickless runners, excepting on very simple courses. On difficult ground the stick-rider strides his pole and takes the slope straight. This is far easier and far swifter than descending by stickless turns and swings. It is also inferior skiing, not because it looks ugly, but because it does not satisfy the only true definition of style, running in that manner which demands least effort and retains most control. The best plan is to disallow the use of sticks. If this is considered too harsh, I would suggest that candidates must carry two sticks and must not put them together and use them as a single pole. For reasons already explained, this would prevent stick-riding.

Skiing Tests

The Roberts of Kandahar Cup has hitherto attracted the best entries of any British skiing competition, and has proved a fine test of skiing. The original course chosen involved a descent of some four thousand feet from the

Wildstrubel hut to Montana over very varied country. The course chosen for this year, the Schilthorn, is about as long and quite as testing a descent. Sticks are allowed in this race, but in time this may be modified.

Skiing tests are also a fruitful subject for discussion. That they have their uses is undeniable. So long as a mild, inoffensive vanity is a tolerably common characteristic of humanity, so long will some sort of recognition of ability stimulate enthusiasm. What would skating be without its tests? Ski-runners are, it is true, far less dependent on tests as a necessary incentive to improvement, but even among ski-runners there is a laudable desire to tabulate one's progress. Tests also serve a useful function in that they differentiate between those who are and those who are not fit to go on an average expedition.

Those who frame skiing tests must bear one cardinal fact in mind. In skating, the turns and figures are an integral part of the sport, and the correct manner in which an unemployed foot should be held is therefore a matter for the most meticulous definition. Now in skiing, the turns and swings are merely a means to an end. The aim of the ski-runner is to get over country as quickly as he can consistent with minimum effort and perfect control of his ski. Therefore a man who can get over the ground at a greater speed and with less effort than another and control his ski equally well is the better runner even if the other candidate can do more swings

On the Level

or performs them in neater style. So that there is no reason why a man should be required to show that he can do a downhill Telemark provided he can come down a difficult course swiftly, steadily, and without undue effort.

Another reason for omitting any specific swings is that they are difficult to judge. The first candidate has undisturbed snow for his manoeuvre, the last candidate has to make his turns in furrowed and beaten snow.

I was on the committee which drew up the B.S.A. Tests, and we kept three things in mind. We wanted to leave as little as possible to the judges, so that the tests should represent a uniform standard in each centre. With this in view, we drafted tests which were little more than a question of timing. The lowest test of all was simply designed to show that a successful candidate was a safe and steady runner. He had to descend fifteen hundred feet in twelve minutes, and over a difficult five-hundred-foot section he was not allowed to fall. He might use his sticks without fear and without reproach. Anybody who passed this test might be trusted to go on an expedition without proving a nuisance. The second-class test was meant to ensure that a successful candidate could run at a very fair speed over ground that would test his powers, and that he had control over his ski and could manage them on difficult ground without stick-riding. The first part of the test was the same as before, with two important differences: the candidate might not fall, and the time was reduced to ten minutes. Further, the candidate had to jump fifteen metres.

A ski-runner who can pass these tests is not necessarily a brilliant runner, but he would show up respectably on tour with good Continental runners, and he can be relied on to run in a free, unhampered style and at a very decent speed.

The first-class test consists in descending fifteen hundred feet in four and a half minutes and jumping twenty-five metres. A ski-runner who could pass this test would be considered a fine performer in any company.

7

An Easter Holiday in Norway

Voksenkollen and the Kjaelka

On 19 March 1909, the following conversation took place: 'Hallo, is that 2630 Avenue? Oh, is that you, Scott? I just rang you up because I'm leaving for Norway in four hours and I thought you might care to join me'. Lindsay, a fellow-member of the Alpine Ski Club, suffers from the not uncommon delusion that he is grievously overworked, and that the machinations of commerce keep him in constant touch with

the City. This theory does not bear the strain
of much investigation, and on this occasion, at
least, commerce was allowed to take care of
itself. Lindsay leapt into a taxi, drove down to
Blackheath, packed violently, and drove up just
in time to catch the train at the Great Central.
Here he took command of the expedition
and thrust me violently into the wrong half
of the train. We were unceremoniously ejected
at a side station, but eventually reached our
boat, the *Montabello*, and set sail on Saturday
morning. Under the genial care of Captain
Cowlrick we had a most enjoyable trip. There
were only seven passengers on board, and we
divided the time between a pianola and long
rambling talks with the captain.

We spent our first night in Norway at
Voksenkollen. Here we passed two delightful
days which we divided between skiing and
the kjaelka. A simultaneous sneeze, hiccough,
and cough give a rough approximation to
the latter word. The kjaelka is a Norwegian
toboggan, longer and narrower than the Swiss
luge, and is steered by a long bamboo eighteen
feet in length. This is trailed on the ground,
and affords a nicety of steering undreamt
of by those who guide with their feet. After
supper Christiania turns out *en masse* and,
duly paired off in couples, makes for the little
restaurant at the top of the favourite kjaelka
run. The conventions of Norwegian society are
delightfully tolerant, though this is a matter of
comparatively recent change. Ski have indeed

revolutionised the social life of Christiania. It is twenty years since the inspiring visit of some Telemark ski-runners drove the youth of Christiania from the café to the hills. Twenty years ago the women of Christiania were of the mid-Victorian type, with no interests outside the family hearth. Then came the ski, and the domestic angel sprouted a pair of wooden wings. To-day the physique of the Christiania women is improved beyond recognition. As a result their mental outlook is enlarged, and they are coming to the fore in questions of policy and education. Ski have played a far larger part than Ibsen in the social revolution.

Skiing at Christiania and its Social Effect

The skiing round Christiania is difficult and mostly consists of wood running. As a result, the best Christiania runners are in a class by themselves. They can take a slope of thirty degrees thickly wooded and turn half-way down to avoid an inconvenient tree. You never see anything but the single furrow, and no good Christiania runner would dream of using his stick. A backward fall is considered a shameful concession to fear, whilst a forward fall is rather an achievement, as it proves that one is running boldly and merely overdoing a good position. 'Ah', said a Norwegian to Lindsay one day, 'you will begin to improve when you learn to fall forward'. Lindsay had just escaped a tree by judiciously falling backwards, so this counsel of perfection left him somewhat cold.

On Wednesday, the 24th, we were joined by Canon Savage, another member of the club, and on Thursday we left for Fefor.

Fefor

Fefor is a fashionable skiing centre—too much so, in fact. The Royal party were skiing there when we arrived, and the manager of our hotel seemed to have all his work cut out to look after them. Such, at least, is the most charitable explanation of certain irritating events. We were annoyed to find that evening dress was worn by many of the guests. One is hardened to this sort of thing in Switzerland, but one expects to escape it in Norway.

Fefor is quite a nice centre. The Fefor Kampa is an ideal little run, but most of the tours suffer from a serious defect. To reach the main range one has nearly an hour's skiing on the level, partly across a lake and partly across long level wooded byways. We made the ascent of the Ruten, the great Fefor expedition, with a party of about eighteen, of whom only one half reached the summit. On this expedition we learned that the average English runner who has had a few seasons in the Alps need not be afraid to join a Norwegian party. The best Norwegian runners are in a class by themselves, which we can never hope to enter, but the ordinary

Easter crowd is nothing to be frightened of, and those who have served an apprenticeship on rough Alpine country will be surprised to see the complicated crabbing with which the average Norwegian attacks a mild gradient. These remarks do not, of course, apply to the best runners. On the slopes round Fofor we used to meet the Royal party, of whom young Prince Olaf has the makings of a promising ski-runner. Owing to the near presence of this party there was an unprecedented demand for accommodation, and the three of us spent our last days in a small room where our tempers and belongings got somewhat mixed, a situation which recalls the remark made to me by a Norwegian at Fefor. This gentleman had a passion for jumping, and could never resist an impromptu hop. On one occasion he landed below a wall, and on rising remarked plaintively that he had 'mixed his contents'.

Tonsaasen

We returned to Christiania at the end of the week and said good-bye to Canon Savage. Lindsay and I then proceeded to Tonsaasen, a delightful centre on the Valdres Railway. We arrived in time for lunch, and in the course of the afternoon had a succession of runs so delightful that we were tempted forth again after dinner. It was dark, and I foolishly took a steep wood run at top speed. My ski caught in the bank, and I fell across the path just as Lindsay's ski caught me in the back. With detached interest I watched Lindsay as he somersaulted gracefully across my prone form, and collected various gems of language from his remarks when he landed some yards farther down.

A Long Trek

Next day we left after lunch and took the train to Aurdal. Here we spent a brisk hour trying to engage a guide. The good lady who runs the local hostel would have proved more useful had she not confined her remarks to the monosyllable 'Yes'. This she volunteered with a fine impartiality to questions of the most conflicting character. For some ten miles we climbed gentle slopes to the edge of a vast plateau that extends for thirty miles of unbroken level. As the sun began to sink we started across one of those long frozen lakes so characteristic of Norway. The twilight lingered on the distant gates of the Jotunheim, and as the sun finally sank a line of fir trees on the edge of a lonely hill was suddenly lit by a glow of magic light. It faded quickly, and the dark, frowning forests were swallowed up by the on-coming night. Across the lake a lonely light heralded the end of the journey. Our guide followed a ski furrow across the snow and led us into the log hut, our resting-place for the night. A cheery log fire was burning in the room where we supped. The only other guest was a Norwegian sailor of genial moods, though his criticism of Lindsay's knife—'You couldn't kill a man with it'—made us careful to shun controversial remarks.

Lindsay and I enjoyed that evening at Market. We felt that we had got away into the wilds. The dress clothes and Royalty of Fefor seemed very far away.

The next day was one of the most trying that I remember. For ten weary hours we slowly trekked through silent sleeping forests, across long white frozen lakes and unbroken deserts of dazzling snow. There was something magnificent in the consistent monotony of the scenery. It never varied. Always the same delicate shades of low-lying hills on our left; the same long, unbroken slopes on our right, pencilled with the faint lines of distant firs; the same interminable plain leaning towards the grey horizon; and far, far ahead the curving of hills beyond.

At Sanderstol we lunched and changed guides. Our new leader was old, stubborn, and lazy. The somewhat transparent device of changing his ski from one foot to the other did not expedite matters. Lindsay set the pace; between us we wedged the guide. I brought up the rear, stamping at intervals on the back of his ski. Four hours from Sanderstol a thin line of smoke climbed above the horizon and marked the position of a small inn, where we had a glass of milk, while Lindsay tried to discover how far we were from Gol by moving the hands of his watch and murmuring 'Gol, Gol, Gol.' Two hours more brought us to the edge of the plain. The sun was softening the twilight snows, and below the valley lay in shadow. It recalled the Rhone Valley on a miniature scale, while beyond it rose a mountain not unlike Monte Leone. In other ranges one looks always for memories of those mountains which claim the first place in our affections.

Twenty minutes of rough skiing brought us to Gol, where a Post-Impressionist sketch of a pig and some eggs produced a very worthy supper. This we should have enjoyed more had our guide not inserted his knife with lordly impartiality first into his mouth, and then into the common stock of butter and marmalade.

Christiania-Bergen Line

We left Gol next morning at 9 a.m. in the Christiania-Bergen train. This railway is one of the finest achievements of engineering. It traverses sixty-two miles of desolate country covered even in the height of summer by frozen lakes and liable even in July to terrible snowstorms. In 1630 an Act was passed forbidding people to cross this no-man's-land between August and May 'for fear of being overtaken by the snow or losing their way'. In winter this grim region might well be the gates leading to the North Pole. The slender railroad seems an impertinent intrusion on the haunts of the Ice-maiden. The line was built under unique difficulties. Numberless sheds had to be erected as a protection against snow-drifts. Avalanches menaced the track and destroyed unprotected portions; blizzards lasting for days drove the workmen to their huts; but courage and determination triumphed, and to-day the traveller gazes from the comfortable seclusion of a dining-car on arctic wastes and uninhabitable snows.

Finse

Finse is situated near the summit of the pass, at a height of four thousand feet above the sea. It consists simply of a hotel, a railway station, and a few workmen's sheds. The hotel had been opened for the first time the day before we came, and we were among the first batch of visitors and the first Englishmen to explore the neighbouring glaciers on ski.

Finse is one of the finest skiing centres in the world. It is within easy reach of some of the finest of Norwegian glaciers. It has an almost inexhaustible range of expeditions, from a two hours' run to a three days' tour. Two club huts facilitate the exploration of neighbouring ranges. During seven months in the year one can put on one's ski at the hotel door and never take them off again till one returns in the evening. During the remaining five months one can reach the perpetual snows of the Hardanger Jokul by a ten-minute row in a boat. In June the skiing is still good, and a big jumping competition takes place towards the end of the month.

Finse lies above the tree-line and offers an uninterrupted succession of open slopes, a joy to the heart of the ski-runner. Half of these enable the ski-runner to run continuously almost to the hotel door; the other half involve ten minutes of level walking across a lake. So much for the skiing qualifications. But apart from these, it was worth coming thus far just to see.

Finse does not possess the strange charm that draws one back year after year to some beloved corner in the Alps. And yet it has a peculiar fascination. There is nothing in the Alps resembling Finse. Let us suppose ourselves on the summit of the Hardanger Jokul, a glacier nev6 two hours from the hotel. A long black line winding among the elbows of the hills is the one link with man. A few minutes more and even the railway has vanished. One is, of course, only playing at danger. Two hours off lies a comfortable hotel, and yet for the moment one can enter into the feelings of a Shackleton leaving his ship for a last dash to the Pole. The view is utterly unlike anything that one sees in the Alps. There, even on the most secluded summits; one sees some trace of life. A cluster of chalets, the green carpet of some cattle-haunted Alp, supply the human interest. Here, on this vast glacier-plateau of the Hardanger Jokul, one seems to be standing at 'the quiet limit of the world'. In an Alpine view there is always some outstanding feature that dominates the landscape. Here it was other- wise. The view depended for its power on no supreme single arresting point, but rather on an impression of organic unity. It had a fascination lacking in the more dramatic phases of the mountain glory, the appeal of such places as the Plaine Morte, where the effect of mystery and power is achieved with a masterly economy of material.

The View from Hardanger Jokul

So from the Hardanger Jokul the eye wanders undisturbed by the presence of any individual grouping of mountain architecture. The absence of trees, of cultivation, of life and colour removed the view from the world in which we move and have our being. Range after range of glacier-capped plateaux dragged themselves out to the grudging grey horizon, dying away with a suggestion of indolent music, only hinting by a suspicion of haze the unseen waters that sleep among their folds. The whole effect is that of a strange, tense dream of, 'Low lands where the sun and moon are quiet and all the stars keep silent'.

From the Hardanger Jokul, which rises to a

height of some six thousand feet, we had some excellent skiing down to the Daemnevand Glacier. We were much impressed by the difficulty of judging distances. In the Alps one soon learns by repeated disappointments to treble the apparent distance of the tantalising sky-line. Here, where the mountains are on a much smaller scale, one soon learns to halve one's estimates, a discovery very soothing to weary limbs.

From Hallingskeid to Ossa

Our last day was in every respect the finest. We left Finse after lunch and took the train to Hallingskeid. Here we put on ski and had a three hours' climb to the pass. It was an irritating ascent, as every successive sky-line towards which we laboriously struggled revealed yet another beyond it. But the pass once reached, our troubles were forgotten.

The appeal of a view depends largely on its contrast with what has gone before, and a prospect that gradually unfolds itself lacks the dramatic power of a sudden revelation from a sky-line. For three hours we had been crossing ridge after ridge, surrounded by the same monotonous, low-lying snows. In one moment the whole character of our outlook changed. We stood at the summit of a slope that curved over with sensational speed, and fell away through five thousand feet of unchallenged steepness to the waters of the Hardanger Fjord. This was frozen for some miles, and I have never seen anything more delicately beautiful than the contrast between the dark silver of the ice and the warm bronze of wider waters melting away into the sunset. We could trace the course of the fjord by the cliffs that barred its unseen reaches. We could trace it for mile after mile till it faded by slow gradations into the mists of twilight, and beyond we could discern—if only with the eye of faith—the salt estranging sea.

> Ich sah im cwigon Abendstrall
> Die stille Welt zu. meine Fiissen
> Entziindet alle Hohn, beruhigt jedes Thai
> Den Silberbach in goldne Strome fliessen.

A Dangerous Pass

For the next hour we had five thousand feet of the most exciting skiing that I can remember. The slope was never less than twenty-five degrees ; it was often more than forty. It was broken up into a series of terraces and sudden dips invisible from above. Through these the guide threaded a careful and skilful path. I was glad to find that I was able to do continuous Alpine turns, thus vindicating this sound manoeuvre, which is somewhat despised by the admirers of more showy swings. Under many conditions this descent must be very dangerous. We saw a magnificent track of a fallen avalanche, and though the snow was good we had one exciting moment. We had to cross a very steep slope. We took it at full speed. Half-way across, the snow began to slip. I kept my balance, and though I side-slipped with the top layer, the pace carried me through with a rush. Lindsay, who followed, had a similar experience.

The Hardanger Fjord

We ran right down to the sea level, and for that matter over the sea itself. At Ossa we started over the frozen fjord. Ossa is a quaint little village almost completely cut off from the outer world when the ice on the fjord does not bear but is just strong enough to stop the passage of a boat. Under such conditions a long and difficult pass is the only means of communicating with the outside world.

Skiing across ice is a wearisome business at the best, yet we forgot our fatigue in the wonder of the twilight. I have never had a lovelier walk. The narrow arm of frozen water, hemmed in by cliffs that swept upwards in abrupt unbroken lines, seemed cut off from the world. Behind us the white walls of our pass slowly rejected the last offices of the sun. The night crept up from the fjord and long, uneasy shadows worked into the elbows of the crags. Above, the silent stars looked out from the sable sky. Across the dark spaces of ice a little light drew nearer, and after an hour of haunting beauty we stepped off on to the shore.

A Wearisome Sleigh-Drive

Three miles across the road brought us to Ulvic, where we said good-bye to our cheery guide. We should have been very glad to spend the night at Ulvic, but I had to be back in England by the first boat, so at midnight we started again on our travels. I had vague hopes of a luxurious sleigh in which one might snatch a furtive sleep. What we actually found was a middle-aged toboggan with a bicycle saddle and a small seat for the driver.

We tossed up for the saddle and I won, so Lindsay sat down on a sort of cross-beam and handed me his legs to take care of. I tucked them under my arms and called upon our charioteer to proceed. A very delicate balance was needed to remain on the sleigh. A vista of moonlit hills filled us with disgust. After two hours the sleigh stopped and we rolled out into the road. The driver had discovered a species of butcher's cart growing like a happy fungus by the roadside. He picked up our sleigh, tossed it carelessly into a ditch, and harnessed the horse on to the cart. We staggered in, rejoicing that at least we had a seat each. I was bored with Lindsay's legs. We tried to snatch a nap, and a great competition for each other's shoulders ended in our two heads meeting with an ugly bump. Another hour or so brought us to a wayside inn, where our driver indicated that we were to change sleighs. I fell asleep across the door, and after a blank eternity somebody dug me up and I climbed wearily into the carriage. I took off my boots and put my feet into the rucksack and, having secured Lindsay's angular shoulder, fell fast asleep. The horse meanwhile seems to have struggled along quite gaily as long as the road led downhill, but at the foot of the first incline he put his ears back and planted his feet forward. The driver roused us, and sulkily we resumed our frozen boots. As we climbed the hill the dawn began to touch the distant snows. I thought of Shakespeare's:

> Night's candles are all out and jocund day
> Stands tip-toe on the misty mountains high

and vaguely wondered where on earth he found anything jocose in a sunrise. At eight o'clock we reached Voss in a shower of rain. Here we breakfasted and quarrelled violently on the subject of ski-bindings. We dozed throughout the day, and kept awake during meals by arguments on Pragmatism. Lindsay, having cornered the absolute, proceeded to contrast the strong, silent, practical Scotsman (C. S. Lindsay) with the weak, noisy, unpractical Irishman (the present writer). Here I fell asleep, and was only awakened when we had to leave the genial warmth of the train for yet another bleak sleigh-drive. At eight p.m. we started across a lake some forty miles long. It was cold, and we were very heartily sick of sleighs. I vaguely remember the full moon rising beyond the white mists of the lake and the black line of sleighs notched into its disk. I seem to recall Lindsay persisting to the last that he was not one of my subjective phenomena, but beyond that I remember little. Somehow those five cold and tedious hours came to an end, and when at length we reached the train we vowed that thirteen hours' sleigh-driving in the day was just thirteen hours too many.

Back to Christiania

We reached Christiania in time for breakfast and spent Good Friday looking forward to bed. For three strenuous days and two equally strenuous nights we had not enjoyed two hours of consecutive sleep. On Saturday we set sail in the Montabello, and our holiday ended, appropriately enough, with a reunion of the original party at Hexham, and—but that is another story.

8

Recollections

Skiing in 1898 | Early Tours at Adelboden | A Primitive Competition | Rickmers and Zdarsky | An Adventure on the Rawyl | The Oberland from End to End | A Storm on the Eiger | The Gspaltenhorn | Conclusion

Skiing in 1898

I put on my first pair of ski in 1898, three years after the first of the classic skiing traverses, Dr Paulcke's crossing of the Oberland. I remember those early skiing lessons very vividly. A few of us, a very few, armed ourselves with ski and repaired to a neighbouring slope. A little group of men with toboggans halted on a path nearby and watched with curiosity. Our instructor, a guide, led off. He slid down the slope leaning heavily on a vast pole, and when he got to the bottom without falling we cheered. He gave us a word of advice: 'Lean on your polo, and if you wish to turn to the right you can come round gradually by putting your stick on the right, and dragging yourself round on it.'. That was in 1898. The few visitors who bothered to ski in Chamounix were regarded as reckless faddists. I was a small boy, and I voted skiing a poor sport. You fell about so. Tobogganing was much simpler and quite as much fun. I don't remember skiing much in the next season, and certainly none of the visitors ever dreamt of going on an expedition. Things were rather livelier in Grindelwald in 1900-1901. The Misses Owen were making some very good tours, but even in Grindelwald an expedition to 'Spion Kop', a little hillock halfway up the Scheidegg, was regarded as a bold and scarcely justifiable venture. Of stemming turns and Telemark swings we were innocent. This is what the author of *A Pleasure Book of Grindelwald* published in 1903, had to say of these new-fangled notions: 'You must hold your legs very firm and use the pole to counteract changes in speed . . . men pretend to have seen Dr Nansen come skiing poleless and at full speed over a glacier, and stop short on the brink of a crevasse by pressing his knees inward so as to press outward against the snow with the soles of his ski. For my part I am willing to wait and begin to cultivate this accomplishment when I have something more than hearsay for a guide'. This was in the days before Caulfeild.

Early Tours at Adelboden

In 1902-1903 I went to Adelboden, and went up my first mountain on ski. To-day the energetic beginner would tackle the Elsighorn and the Laveigrat in his first week. There is a broad track up the Laveigrat, and you may sometimes see fifty beginners on its slopes. Things were different in 1902. Our guide told us we were the first party up the Elsighorn on ski, which may or may not have been true, but certainly I cannot remember more than two other parties that made long tours.

To the sophisticated runner the results of that season may seem rather barren. I went up the Elsighorn with Mr Percival Earrar and broke a ski on the top. The Laveigrat we climbed after four days of rain, followed by a forty-degree frost. In all the years I, have skied I have never seen a summer grass mountain covered from head to foot in ice, not hard frozen snow, but an icy surface on which we left absolutely no track. A ridiculous incident occurred on the descent. On a slope which a beginner could take straight without fear, I slipped and fell. I was, of course, on foot—the snow was utterly un-skiable—and I was soon shooting down head first and on my back. The guide was some distance ahead, and he threw himself in my path. My head was driven through my body and emerged some- where in the region of my toes, and the guide was badly winded. His wrist was also sprained. On my third climb, the

Schwandfehlspitze, I joined Canon Savage and parted company with a boot. I was rubbing frozen feet in snow at the time, and the guide's remarks when, after a two hours' search, he returned with the errant footgear were well worth hearing.

Three expeditions and practically no skiing. Well, somehow we did not look on it in that light. In those days we seem to have climbed a hill as much for the view and the joy of new country as for the run home, an attitude which may appear odd to the sophisticated runner. Certainly I carried back with me the feeling that a new beauty had entered into life, and the memory of my first view from a winter mountain is not lightly forgotten.

A Primitive Competition

The standard of skiing in that the first Adelboden winter may be judged from the race for the Public Schools Alpine Sports Challenge Cup. The competitors were told to ski round a certain field. I fancy there was about 100 feet of actual descent. The rest was mere trudge. The winner staggered round the course in some five minutes, and only fell twice. Next year the competitions were a little more genuine, thanks to Rickmers. There was some 300 feet of descent and a long climb. Twenty competitors entered, and I was lucky enough to win, beating Lowe, the Worcestershire cricketer, who was second.

I was rather pleased with myself at the time, but on considering it in the light of later years my victory is an eloquent testimony to the low standard of our skiing. I am quite sure I could never have got through the lowest test of the British Ski Association.

That was the state of affairs in the season of 1902-1903. And lest we forget what is owing to Rickmers, it is only fitting to compare the darkness which he found with faith as he left it.

Rickmers and Zdarsky

Rickmers put on his first pair of ski in 1900 under the tutelage of Zdarsky. Zdarsky was and is a very remarkable man. He is something of a philosopher, and has lived for many years a hermit life in Lilienfeld, near Vienna. He has never allowed any one to serve him. He built the house in which he lives, and is his own cook and housemaid. 'As a genius of expedients and makeshifts', writes Air. Rickmers, 'he can have but few rivals, combining as he does something of the craft of the savage with the practical knowledge of modern engineering received at a technical college. I should not be surprised to see him light a fire with ice or find a drink in the hottest Hades'. Zdarsky had a difficulty in obtaining stores owing to the deep snow in winter, and having read of ski, he sent to Norway for a pair. Now the ordinary Norwegian ski with the cane bindings are not easily managed save by an expert, and Zdarsky was neither an export nor had he any expert to put him on the right way. He applied the inventive mind of which Rickmers speaks and set about analysing the dynamics of skiing. He rediscovered some part of what was already known, and not unnaturally failed to rediscover much that was already known. He has the credit of writing the first systematic exposition of skiing, in which he naturally enough claimed as his own invention the stemming turn which he had discovered independently, but which, as a matter of fact, had formed part of the instinctive knowledge of Norwegians for generations. The book is remarkable for many things. Zdarsky is something of a genius, and his exposition of skiing is clear-headed and shows a real grip of the complicated dynamics of the sport. If Zdarsky had been a little less sure of himself, if he had been taught by a Norwegian expert, if he had not been so profoundly convinced that he was making great and original discoveries, if there had been half as much of the disciple as of the prophet in his nature, his book might well have been the finest and most able treatise on the sport in existence. The Lilienfeld technique, as he called it, might have passed through the usual cycle. If Zdarsky had been a trifle more humble he would have welcomed criticism, and perhaps modified the faults of his system. But, unfortunately, the Viennese are born hero-worshippers. They idolised Zdarsky, and confirmed him in his own conviction that he had hit upon something very new and very remarkable in skiing. Every Sunday they came in crowds from Vienna, and Zdarsky marshalled them on the hill-sides with the zeal of a schoolmaster and the iron discipline of a Prussian drill sergeant. Zdarsky had the Teutonic love for teaching folk and for organising his pupils. 'No one was spared the well-deserved snub for naughtiness or cheek' and those who liked to be treated as schoolboys enjoyed the advantage of gratuitous tuition and the simple hospitality of Habernreith.

Unfortunately the matter did not end there Zdarsky's pupils made the unfounded claim that his technique was a new invention and an improvement on anything that had ever come from Norway. As was to be expected, the challenge was taken up, and for many seasons a royal 'battle of the bindings' supplied skiing magazines with some spirited copy. Paulcke led the disciples of the Norwegian school and Rickmers took up the cudgels for Zdarsky, and if their respective followers could have burned each other at the stake, I dare say they would have cheerfully done so. The controversy came to an end in 1905. The Norwegian Ski Association sent over a representative to Vienna, who soon made friends with Zdarsky. The Litienfelders were struck with the dash and command of Zorn's running, and Zorn himself was not a little impressed by Zdarsky's method of teaching novices. 'The peace of Vienna,' as Richardson calls it, healed the controversy.

In 1903-1904, when Rickmers came to Adelboden, the battle was at its height. Personally I do not like the Lilienfeld technique. I started skiing two years before Rickmers, and I was never a pupil of his. In my blundering fashion I tried to practise straight running rather than continual stemming turns, and I stuck to my Norwegian ski, though to be seen without a pair of Lilienfeld ski on one's feet was to stamp oneself as an out-and-out heretic. But though I think

Dawn among the High Alps

that Zdarsky taught a bad style, yet I hold that English skiing is perhaps more indebted to his disciple, Rickmers, than to any other ski-runner. Even Caulfeild, who has said some very hard things about the system, gladly acknowledges his debt to its leading exponent, and few of us who were skiing in the early days but retain kindly memories of long days on the hills marked out by the enthusiasm which Rickmers threw into every detail of the expedition. The question is not what style he taught. Opinions vary on the merits of his system. The point to be remembered is that he found Adelboden given over to skating and other mischievous practices. In my first season there were only two or three parties who even ventured as far as the Hahnenmoos. Rickmers, by sheer force of enthusiasm, drew away crowds from the rink and the toboggan run. Old men and maidens were coerced into learning the new art, and a broad and beaten track soon led to the old solitudes of the Hahnenmoos. If he did not teach a dashing style, he at least inspired many with a love for the mountains and a respect for their dangers. He turned out good winter mountaineers, if he did not produce first-class runners.

Adventure on the Rawl

After a few winters of easy tours I had my first taste of winter mountaineering at Montana.

The dangers of the winter Alps bear little relation to the size of the peaks. The summer mountaineer soon learns that he can get into serious trouble in a region of small mountains. This fact was impressed on me long ago by a certain incident on a summer mule-path.

Early in January 1908, having explored our route thoroughly in summer, I left Montana to cross the mountains to Villars. My companion, Mr Wyberg, had only been on ski three times, but he was a mountaineer of considerable experience. We climbed without incident to the Plaine Morte, where we parted. Wyberg went on to the hut, while I crossed the glacier and climbed the Wildstrubel. When the sun had set I hurried down to the glacier, and reached it just as night fell.

Even in daylight the Plaine Morte has a curious spell. To the uninitiated it may seem a vast expanse of featureless snow, but for others it is the last refuge of mystery. Its effect of size is heightened by the insignificance of the bounding wall, low-lying slopes of shale and scree that secrete its recesses from the curious greeting glances of the greater hills. Its snows are as deceptive as the sea, and the weary traveller has nothing whereby to measure progress. And that night I was soon overwhelmed by a sense of monotonous distance. The fact that I was alone and tired added to the uncanny disquiet of my surroundings. A bitter wind blew over the glacier and threatened frostbite. I trekked onwards through the night, but never seemed to get any nearer the hut. The world seemed dead and I its sole inhabitant. Nothing was visible, nothing save long reaches of mysterious snows, and the dark curving of great hills dimly suggested beyond the shadowed wall. The Dead Plain stretched away into the darkness with all the intolerable monotony of a nightmare. Monotonous surroundings have a deadening effect on tired limb and body. I tried the useless device of counting steps: five hundred—the Gletcherhorn had not moved; a thousand—and I seemed no farther from the Wildstrubel.

A steady sequence of thuds disturbed me. Wyberg was chopping wood outside the hut, four miles away. Somehow the weary iteration of that sound irritated me intensely. The faint thuds beat a tedious rhythm in my brain and had much the same effect as the Inquisition torture, a steady sequence of water drops on the victim's head. Between the monotony of the plain and the monotony of that sound I soon gave way to those odd fancies that haunt the border-line between waking and sleep. Somehow or other the hut was reached, though I have no clear memory of the last hour, which seems to have been chiefly occupied in resisting the temptation to lie down and sleep.

The night was bitterly cold, and as the hut was neither wind- nor snow-proof (a new hut has since been built which is very comfortable) we suffered great discomfort. Our proper route lay over the summit of the Wildhorn, but for various reasons we determined to take a short cut down to Lenk. The *Alpine Club Guide* assured us that the Rawyl Pass was a mule-path in summer, and so we decided to make for Lenk via the Rawyl. Our subsequent experience was a valuable lesson. We learned how little summer information is to be depended on in winter, and how a mere mule-path may become a dangerous trap.

Owing to various delays we did not leave the hut till 12.30 p.m. We ran down to the head of the cliffs along which the Rawyl path climbs. I had some difficulty in finding the bridle track, but discovered it by making for some *Zufluchthütte* marked on the map. One of the guides was badly frostbitten. We shouldered our ski and hurried down to a point where the path turned a sharp corner. This corner of the path was cut out of the face of the precipice, and in summer we should have passed it without comment. As we found it the wind had driven the snow into an icy hank of extraordinary steepness abutting on to a precipice. I was leading at the time, and started making steps with the greatest carefulness. An ice-axe would have been invaluable. The steps had to be kicked into the hard surface, and there was some risk of the snow-bank slipping and carrying us with it. After the steps had been made the ski had to be handed over, a lengthy proceeding. Meanwhile the sun had begun to set. We realised that a night on the mountain was becoming a probable contingency. Another long stretch and another corner brought us to a point where Wyberg thought that we might escape by a couloir, so we wearily ploughed down some three hundred feet, only to find that the couloir ended in a precipice. That did not please us, nor were the search party who followed us two days later delighted by this detour, which they followed with meticulous thoroughness. Owing to some very bad bungling, a telegram addressed to my father never reached him, and a search party was despatched from Montana. They followed our tracks over the Rawyl, and were much impressed by the danger and stupidity of the route.

The situation was gloomy. We had to climb back to the path through the deep snow, ski on our back. There was little daylight left, and the night was rushing up from the valley. We found afterwards on comparing notes that we had both selected an eligible rock under which to spend the night, but we determined to make a last dash for safety. When we reached the path it amused itself by disappearing in a gully. We crossed this with anxiety, as it leant over into space and seemed composed of snow at a very dangerous angle. We had crossed the gully and turned the last corner when the last rays of light failed. 'The stars rush out, at one stride comes the dark'.

But we had won our race by a head. Below us stretched a long unbroken slope of snow leading down to the Iffigen Valley; bed and dinner were merely a matter of time. That night was the coldest of the winter and, all things considered, we were lucky to win through.

The remaining two days provided easy and delightful skiing over low-lying passes, and I have recalled this expedition not because it was an achievement of which I am in any sense proud, but because it illustrates the danger of summer routes in winter. The accidental details of the search party gave it a regrettable notoriety, and the choice of the dangerous Rawyl as a skiing route was severely criticised by a well-known Swiss mountaineer in the Lausanne Gazette. The subsequent correspondence brought me into touch with Professor Roget, and next winter (January 1909) we planned and carried through a very successful ski tour.

I propose to give a short description of it in the hope that many English runners may be induced to follow in our tracks. The opening of the Jung-frau Railway as far as the Jungfrau-Joch brings the Aletsch snowfield within easy reach of the ski- runner, and British runners have no excuse for neglecting these magnificent glaciers, so well known to Continental runners.

The Oberland from End to End

Our object was to cross the Oberland from end to end by a high-level route. Part of this route, the great glacier highway from Ried to Meiringen, has long been a favourite with foreign runners. We started from Kandersteg, and after crossing the Petersgrat joined this route at Kippel. We found the best guides engaged, and we had to put up with a guide and two porters, none of whom were good runners and one of whom was the worst runner and porter that I have ever met. Schmid and Gyger are now both good ski-ing guides. Adolph, I trust, has returned to his Gasternthal inn. He should never have left it.

We left Kandersteg on January 2 at 5.30 a.m. Three hours later we reached Adolph's inn. He suggested that we had done enough for glory and that after refreshments we should return. He had joined in the festivities which welcomed in the new year, and shortly after leaving the inn he collapsed. This he explained was due to asthma—an elegant euphemism. The guides contemptuously divided up his load and dubbed him the Socialist. *'Sehr sehr müde'* was the burden of his refrain during the hours that followed.

Throughout this and the following days we took things very easily. The secret of a successful winter tour is to plan out your day so as just to reach the hut in time for supper. The halts should be at regular intervals, and the pace throughout should be consistent with reaching the hut in the desired time. You thus arrive perfectly fresh, having enjoyed to the full the glories of your surroundings. Some such scientific laziness adds enormously to the pleasure of these long day climbs. We took fourteen hours where a fast party might take eleven to reach the hut. The last three hours of our journey lay along the névé of the Tschingel glacier. The sunset was soon followed by the rise of the full moon, a moon undreamt of in our English skies. The bare statement that I could read with ease the smallest print in a notebook gives a very inadequate idea of the contrast between the radiant glory of that January moon and the pale spectre that 'hurries with unhandsome thrift of silver' across English skies. Every fissure in the snow, every winkle on the cliffs, was revealed by her critical rays. From the pass the Jungfrau rose above a sea of shadows backed by the balanced pyramid of the Eiger. The moonlight slept on her snowy terraces and steeped her cliffs in incarnate light. The hut stood in a circle of snow. Here the wind had played strange havoc, torturing the billows and cornices of snow into a mosaic of coloured lights.

The next day we crossed the Petersgrat in eight hours to Kippel. Our guides took us a bad route along the western slopes of the Telli glacier. Last winter I saw from the Breithorn the proper route, which lies down the western slopes of the Grindel glacier. This gives excellent running on the eastern snow, and it is possible by this route to go direct from the Mutthorn to the Lötschenlücke in one day. As it was, we had some very bad running, and a nasty half-hour in a risky couloir.

Next day we left Kippel—Reid is shut in winter—at 6 a.m. The Lötschenlücke, our goal, is an ideal pass. It is the obvious gap at the head of a long valley, from almost every point of which it is visible. It simply cries out to be crossed. The delicate curve of the pass, slung between mountain barriers and backed by great depths of blue, haunts you throughout the day with all the magic of the sky-line.

I shall not forget that walk up the Lötschenthal. We stopped for breakfast in some cheese-making huts and exchanged mild banter with the owners thereof. Six hours from Kippel we reached the first of those glaciers which we did not leave for three days. We had the whole day to reach the hut, and there was no temptation to hurry. Slowly the distant ranges climbed into a larger sky. Slowly the upward track gained on the pass. The morning melted into the noon, and the afternoon into the evening. We paused below the final slope to watch the glow creeping up the slopes of Mont Blanc far away in the west. Even the guides were impressed by the strange stillness as

> Light and sound ebbed from the earth,
> Like the tide of the full and -weary sea
> To the depths of its own tranquillity.

Then, as the night fell, we turned upwards towards the sky-line, whose promise had haunted us throughout the day. All through the long hours we had been climbing with our faces turned towards the slope, and our hearts set on the final revelation. Now only a few yards remained. We took them at a rush. The Finsteraarhorn shot out above the ridge. The pass was made.

The rays of the risen moon blended with the ebbing twilight and lent an atmosphere of mystery to the great 'urns of the silent snows' from which the king of Alpine glaciers draws strength. It was my first view of the Aletsch, and the moment was full of a certain personal romance. The portals of the pass became a magic casement opening on to perilous snows 'mid faery lands folorn'.

The Egon von Steiger hut is some twenty minutes above the pass. Adolph, with a fine sense for the fitness of things, chose the moment when supper was on the table to put in a belated appearance. A great appearance of bustle and a hole burnt in my socks were the contributions he made to the evening labour.

We left next morning shortly after six, and had some tricky roped skiing in the dark. Adolph would seat himself, and four rapid jorks would bring the rest of the party into like positions. We decided that 'there was a good deal to be said for being dead' if the alternative was more of this roped skiing, so we cast off the cord. Nor did we again resume it while on ski, a fact which lays us open to criticism. We had a look at the Jungfrau, but decided against attempting it, and proceeded instead over the Grunhornlücke, which involved a climb of about an hour from the Concordia. These six days on ski stand out as the story of four sky-lines opening on to new worlds of spacious wonder. There had been the Petersgrat with its sudden prospect over the great guardian of the Lötschenthal, the Lötschenlücke with its revelation of the Aletsch, the Grunhornlücke from which we looked down on to the Fiesch glacier, and the last of our passes which opened on to the Oberaar glacier and the peaks beyond the Grimsel. There is some spell that haunts the humblest of sky-lines, and to me these four passes with their revelation of unknown snow proved by far the chiefest joy of these great and lasting days.

We lay on the summit of the pass and enjoyed a prolonged siesta in the snow. The temperature was that of an Italian spring. We joyfully contrasted our easy journeys with the summer tramp through slushy clinging snow.

We reached the Finsteraarhorn hut after eight easy hours.

As we settled down to supper a party of guideless Swiss, fine strapping fellows characteristic of the large class that spend their week-ends among the mountains, returned from the Finsteraarhorn, our goal for the morrow.

On Wednesday, January 6, we left the hut at 6.30 in the morning. Adolph was taken, as he wished to come, but we pointed out that he was to consider himself as a passenger. We climbed steep slopes of snow, varied by patches of ice, to the Hugisattell, from which there descended the most alarming ski tracks that I have ever seen. Two Norwegians had climbed the Finsteraarhorn, taking ski to within a thousand feet of the summit, and had gaily skied down a slope of snow, varied by streaks of ice, at an angle of forty-five degrees, an occasional crevasse no doubt adding incident to their run. We climbed and descended this slope on a rope.

Four and a half hours after leaving the hut we breakfasted on the Hugisattell, a little gap overlooking the slioer cliff that falls to the Finsteraarhorn glacier. Thence we proceeded to attack the last arête. Adolph's weary plaint, *'Ich komme sehon aber nur nicht zu schnell'* fell on unsympathetic ears. We kept to the very edge of the ridge. The rocks were delightfully warm and easy, and from start to finish the climb was no harder than in summer.

That last ridge of the Finsteraarhorn is one of the finest things in the Alps. Drop a stone and it falls 3000 ft. without a bound. There is nothing half so sheer on the Matterhorn as that plunge down to the glaciers above Grindelwald.

At last, at half-past one, we reached the zenith of our long journey. I have never seen guides so unfeignedly delighted. Even the cynic of the party caught some of the prevailing enthusiasm. We suffered slightly from the heat, and I relieved myself by stripping to the waist and wallowing in the snow. Adolph composed himself to slumber, and the rest of us sat about in shirt-sleeves.

The view is of its kind unique. We were in the centre of vast spaces of eternal winter. Below, the great cliffs of the Oberland scarrod by the writing of the ages rose from a waste of glaciers. The Finsteraarhorn is the highest point of the chain, and looks defiantly over a host of lesser peaks to its great brethren of the Central Alps. A boundless canopy of clouds covered the lowlands of three nations, dragging itself out to the low horizon and breaking in waves of light on the Rigi and the hills of the Black Forest in the north, on the terraces of Lombardy in the south. No breath of wind broke in upon the inviolable quietness.

> It seemed as if the hour were one
> Sent from beyond the skies.
> Which scattered from above the sun
> The light of Paradise.

That windless hour seemed stolen from the passage of Time. Old memories rose unbidden. The far-off greeting of familiar ridges, the hills of Grindelwald, from which as small boys we had Lifted longing eyes to the greater peaks, and the little chalet of those early years, all helped to awaken memories of 'far-off things and battles long ago'.

The hour passed like ten minutes. We roused Adolph, and sadly turned downwards. The weaker brother was lowered down the ridge with great deliberation, but there were compensations for his slowness. It was a strange experience to sit astride that vast cliff and watch the shadows creeping down the snows at our feet, and the canopy of mist responding to the afternoon lights. We did not hurry, and reached the hut at 5.45 p.m.

On our last day we left at 7 a.m. and crossed the Oberaarjoch. The glacier of the same name gave us some splendid skiing, and we had good running the whole way to the Grimsel, whore we found the traditional winter. Above, on the glaciers all had been warmth, colour, and light. Here in this grim gorge all was grey and chill. The deserted post road was gagged with old avalanche runs and overhung with icicles. Below, the angry torrent loomed out between cakes of sullen ice, whilst the waning light cast cold shadows on sombre bosses of grey rock.

We ran down the road to our journey's end at Guttanen, having enjoyed some 9000 feet of skiing from our pass to the village. The hotel was closed, but we found rooms for the night in an adjoining chalet. We supped in the one room which was warmed. The patriarch was mumbling in the corner over his pipe. The father chatted amiably of the winter work cutting the wood and bringing it down to the valley. A small boy was doing his school tasks, a girl and her mother were sewing and spinning, and the youngest scion of the house was asleep on the stove. It was one of those glimpses of the real life of the industrial Swiss that the summer visitor so seldom sees.

On Friday we were up again before the dawn, and drove into Meiringen. A pedantic desire to finish the journey on ski was compromised by tailing behind the sleigh, and our long journey came to an end on the platform at Meiringen six days and six hours after leaving Kandersteg.

We had crossed four glacier passes, slept four nights above the snow-line, and climbed the Finsteraarhorn. We had passed through the finest scenery in the Alps, and all this had involved no discomfort and practically no strain. Under such conditions winter mountaineering is an easy and simple matter, involving neither difficulty nor danger. Anybody of ordinary physique and three weeks' skiing experience could follow in our footsteps without difficulty, risk, or discomfort. The number of British runners making such expeditions remains deplorably few, and if this book removes the false impression that British runners have formed of the difficulty of these glacier tours, these lines will not have been written in vain. That Easter I went to Norway, and my experiences there are the subject of another chapter.

In the summer I came away with some rotten rock on a Welsh climb, and shattered my leg. I had the good luck to have Mr Warren, who is on the staff of the London Hospital, within easy reach, and though amputation seemed probable, he somehow managed to mend my leg, which was crushed, and broken in numberless fragments. I lay on my back for four months, and at the end of eighteen I could just walk four miles without collapsing. I thought that I could probably ski, and Mr Warren gave me permission to try. So I left for the Alps wondering whether a leg two inches short, a stiff ankle, and a running wound would make skiing impossible.

The morning after my arrival I put on ski and shuffled along the level sick with suspense. Roget was teaching some beginners on a mild slope, and when I slid clumsily down it he raised a cheer which startled his pupils, who doubtless thought it an ironic tribute to the elaborate precautions with which I lowered myself down the snow.

Various good people told me that I was a fool, but Warren's advice was sound. Every time I fell forward adhesions in my toes and ankle wore ruthlessly broken down, a cheap and simple form of massage. By the end of the season my ankle was comparatively loose, and my muscles were worked up to a decent strength.

I managed to struggle up the Dent Blanche in the following summer, and this encouraged me to engage Crettex for the winter of 1911-1912. Crettex is quite a hero at Champex, and perhaps the finest of all skiing guides. He is a man of splendid physique, and I shall never forget the impression he made on me when I first saw him. I was a boy of fifteen on the way to my first snow climb, and Crettex strolled into the hut with the graceful swagger that recalled Leslie Stephen's description of Lauoner. Crettex is a real lover of the hills, and has often stopped to point out with keen delight some sudden effect of mist and snow. He is a man of forty, yet even on the humblest expedition he reveals the enthusiasm of a boy on his first climb; and, unlike some guides paid by the day, he is desperately keen to put in as much climbing as possible. Two years ago he met with an accident. A trap swung round the corner of a narrow Alpine road and crushed him against a wall. With all the force of his marvellous physique he thrust the carriage from him and carried away a part of the wall. That lost him a season's climbing.

I met him at Champex shortly after he had left the hospital. I had hobbled up on my game leg, and so for me our meeting had a certain significance. It was a terrible shock to find the wreck of a great guide sitting by the mule-path. '*Je regrette beaucoup mes montagnos.*' I could understand, the sorrow behind those simple words, and share in a measure his great joy when he won his way back to the hills. He celebrated his complete recovery by leading Rogot up the Dent Blanche in January.

He joined me in December of last year at Campfer, and our first venture was hardly a success. We had sleighed to Maloja, and started thence for the Forno hut at about three in the afternoon. As the night fell Crettex showed some anxiety, and at half-past ten I consulted the map once more and hazarded a guess that we were at least a thousand feet too high. The lady of the party remarked cheerfully, 'I suppose if we don't find the hut we shall have to dig a hole and sleep in the snow'. To my unromantic temperament there seemed something to be said for the miseries of a roof, so I despatched Crettex to search for the hut. His lantern flickered among the rocks and vanished in the darkness. Meanwhile Miss B., her brother, and I sat on a rock and possessed our souls impatience. As the time passed and the temperature fell we gradually tended

towards the Euclidean definition of a solid
body, 'that which moveth altogether if it move
at all'. The wind began to whisper among the
hills. Grey masses filled the hollows, the white
gleam of the glacier peered between trailing
mists. Orion darted behind a curtain of mist,
and with soft treacherous movement the snow
began to fall. At midnight Crettex returned in
despair, and we decided to make for one of the
cowsheds below the glacier.

We rattled down to the glacier and, selecting
an eligible rock, proceeded to dine—a wise
precaution, for food represents warmth,
energy, and courage when one is faced by an
awkward situation. It was an odd setting for a
meal. Crettex hung his lantern on an axe, and
we washed down frozen chicken with frozen
milk while the old grey ghosts that follow the
mist moaned uneasily round the hills.

Of the strain of that descent through the
snow and the night two things stand out,
Miss B.'s pluck and Crettex' skill in picking
up the half-obliterated tracks. We reached our
haven just before two, an odd little cow-chalet.
The floor was damp and muddy, the wall was
pierced by occasional windows innocent of
glass, and the architect seems to have been
blind to the advantage of a chimney. A bunk
with a straw mattress would have been more
desirable had it not been placed just beneath
one of the aforesaid windows, which obligingly
welcomed such gusts of wind-blown snow as
sought shelter. Crettex worked like a hero all

night, and I can still see his Rembrandtesque outline as he hurled branch after branch on the fire. The grey light of dawn found us exceedingly weary, but, as far as Miss B. was concerned, still cheerful, '*Tonnerre quelle mademoiselle solide!*,' was Crettex' verdict.

A Storm on the Eiger

Crettex and I went on to the Oberland and, wearied by constant bad weather, set out for the Eiger, hoping that the luck would change. We left the Eiger station at 2.30 and zigzagged up the snow slopes that lead to the base of the rocks. As a boy I had read with absorbing interest Tuckett's account of his race for life from the avalanche that is still a danger of this route. We left our ski some distance below the rocks, and about forty minutes later we were startled by a sudden sharp report. We looked up at the ice wall just below the Klein Eiger, just as the thunder of falling ice crashed down on to the sleeping snows. With a venomous hiss the avalanche spread out on the slopes to a breadth of some three hundred yards and filled the cliffs with the echoes of its anger. It seemed strangely sinister in the waning moonlight as it forced its way downwards to the shadowed depths. Crettex filled the night with lamentations for his lost ski, a small sacrifice to the malice of the Eiger.

Meanwhile the weather had turned bad; a trailing mist swept down from the Monch and it began to snow. On reaching the rocks I very soon discovered that nailed Laupaars are worse than useless on iced and glazed slabs. I slid about in the most helpless fashion. There was no time to bother about style, so we adopted a method of progress which soon proved very wearisome. Crettex, secure on his crampons, dashed upwards, and I followed scrambling after him, snatching at glazed holds and balancing with the aid of my axe. If I stuck to the rocks, so much the better; if not, there was always the rope. Those long hours fade into one blurred picture. Always the same dull foreground of grey icy slabs leaning upwards into the greyness, the same soft insistent snow-fall, and the same unending monotony of insecure scrambling, varied by violent wrenches as I swung round on the rope.

The pageant of the storm was worth some risk. The fair-weather traveller never sees those sudden changes when a giant hand tears aside the curtain and reveals some black scowling pinnacle half masked by driving snow. Sometimes our path led to the very edge of that great curtain of cliff which falls through six thousand feet of dizzy depths to the peaceful pastures of the Scheidegg. To gaze down where dark ice-fretted crags stooped to an unceasing strife of wind-tormented, battling clouds, to catch through a furtive gap in the ranks of mist some vision of quiet snows far below, is to feel the solemn might of the mountains as is only possible when 'the furies are in mad hunt along the ridges' There is a peculiar challenge in the thought of victory snatched from superior forces, a certain romance in the wavering issue of a hard-fought struggle against storm and weariness.

We had been climbing for nearly eight hours when the final ice slope loomed out of the mist. It involved more than an hour's step-cutting. At 11.45, nine and a quarter hours after starting, Crettex and I shook hands on the summit. We turned immediately and started down the arête. Suddenly a stone leapt out into the air and whistled past like a shell. A gale swept down on to the ridge and hurled me out of my stops. As I swung round against the slope I caught a sudden picture of Crettex, every muscle in his magnificent frame braced tense to meet the shock. I struggled back into the steps and was twice again thrown out. Crettex tells me he has never been in such a storm. Somehow or other I managed to regain my balance to work carefully down till the rope ran out. Crettex asked me in an agonised voice if I was *solide*. I was anything but *solide*, but I leant back against the hurricane while he joined me. My eyes were gummed up with ice and the steps were hidden by driven snow. The wind whipped the loose fragments of ice off the slope and lashed them against our faces. The rope blew out between us like a sail. I had to sound with my axe for the unseen steps, which had been cut uncomfortably far apart. Hungrily we looked down at the little rib of rocks, the haven of safety. Yard by yard we fought our way down and across that icy staircase. At such moments one experiences an odd sense of detachment. At the first onslaught of the storm I felt fear in the pit of my stomach, but the fury of its attack soon exhausted all strong emotions. I seemed to be watching with mild curiosity an interesting conflict between the Eiger in evil humour and two depressed climbers. Not till we flung ourselves breathless and exhausted on the rocks did I really savour the full force of that tense and crowded half-hour. Above us the cliffs still answered to the gale. 'That was no badinage,' said Crettex, with a grim smile.

Six inches of snow on iced rocks made me envy more than ever tho security of Crettex in his crampons, and I vowed never to climb a mountain again without a pair. Somehow we managed to descend without further incident. We swore mildly when we found two broken ski and no trace of Crettex' pair. I did not enjoy trudging down to Wengen, which I reached after eighteen and a half weary hours.

The Gspaltenhorn

Our next climb was the Gspaltenhorn. We wandered up the lonely Kienthal to the Griesalp Hotel, which had been opened for our benefit. Next day we climbed to the Gamchi-balm club hut. The weather was threatening and there seemed little chance of success on the morrow. I shall never forget the jolly way in which Crettex came out that night in the hut. I smoked pipe after pipe and listened while he unfolded strange tales of desperate scrambles in storm and sunshine, of *demoiselles* who fainted on the top of the Matter- horn and of their subsequent carrying down from the summit to the 'Shoulder', of cowardly guides who wept when the hurricane descended, of porters who talked plaintively of wife and child, of Crettex' magnificent retort, *'Ici on ne cause pas de femmes, on cause de roc hers'*, of hasty disappearances over the passes into Italy to escape military service, and of the fortnight in prison at Sion with which Crettex cheerfully winds up the summer season. All this and much more he told with strange chuckles, curious and tempered oaths, and a wealth of magnificent gesture.

Next morning the weather reformed and we had a merry scramble up the Gspaltenhorn, which had only once been climbed in winter. As Oberland peaks go it may be considered difficult, and there were one or two obstacles that gave us pause. Next day we parted, and shortly afterwards I left for England. At Basle I changed my mind and returned to Mürren, where I found Edward Tennant preparing for the Lauterbrunnen Breit-horn. He asked me to join him. He had engaged two local guides, Von Allmen and Feuz, who assured us that the mountain had not been climbed in winter—a fact which may or may not have been true. Contrary to the advice of his guides, I persuaded him to take crampons.

We left next day for the Mutthorn hut, and experienced intense cold. The thermometer showed over forty degrees of frost Fahrenheit, and the surface of my wound was caked with frozen blood, a condition of affairs that brought a bad attack of pain. The glory of the moonlit snows quite staggered Tennant and recalled my first visit to the hut.

Next morning we left at five, and were all but frostbitten by the time we reached the arête. This intense cold is quite abnormal in winter climbing. I put on crampons at once, but Tennant's guides persuaded him that he would not require them. We had a long and interesting climb up the ridge, and Tennant, who had chosen this stiff expedition for his first big climb, seemed to take quite naturally to the best methods of climbing snow-covered rocks. We reached the summit after eight hours, and I made the guides put on Tennant's crampons, a fact which made all the difference to his comfort on the summit of the ice slope and considerably steadied him lower down. After a perfect sunset on the Petersgrat we ran down to the hut, and next day returned to Mürren.

The possibility of midsummer skiing has been proved more than once, and the Jungfrau Railway has removed the chief objection, namely, the difficulty of transporting the ski to the summer snow-line. This summer, with Egon Hessling, a member of the French Alpine

Club, I made a tentative experiment with ski. We carried our ski and our persons to the Jungfrau-Joch station, which lies at the head of the great Aletsch glacier. We found the snow in excellent condition, and our ski proved of great service as far as the steep slope which leads to the Rottal Sattel. The Jungfrau was in very good condition and we climbed it without incident. Our original plan was to ski down to the Concordia, whence we hoped to climb the Finsteraarhorn, but a sudden onslaught of bad weather forced us to beat a hasty retreat. We were without guides, and we had quite an exciting time before we recovered our old tracks which led back to the Jungfrau-Joch. Though we had very little actual skiing, this experience convinced me that there is a great opening for the use of ski in summer, especially in the Oberland, where the Jungfrau line removes the chief obstacle to the sport.

Conclusion

Let me conclude this chapter by urging once again that these long winter climbs involve no peculiar peril and make little demands on strength. In the fourteen winters during which I have made skiing tours I have only twice been in serious danger: once on the Rawyl, owing to a stupid mistake, and once on the Eiger, where we asked for trouble by climbing in bad weather. Few people can have hunted or motored for so long with as little suspicion of peril. The truth is that, though the man who can lead up the Grepon or the Brenva Mont Blanc must possess unusual nerve, strength, and talent, ordinary mountaineering between guides in summer or winter is open to the humblest worshipper of the sovereign heights. We whose physical disabilities cut us off from the enjoyment of other sports can never be too grateful that even the halt may sometimes pass the silent gateways of the snows. In other sports all the prizes fall to the expert. The mountains show a more royal carelessness in their favours, and though they keep their best for the bolder lover, yet even for us there is, in the words of an old traveller, 'no high hill which doth not contane in it some most sweete memorie of worthy matters'.

Appendix

FARES BY SHORTEST SEA ROUTE

	1st Single			2nd Single			1st Retrn.			2nd Retrn.		
	£	s.	d.	£	s.	d.	£	s.	d.	£	s.	d.
Argentière *via* Martigny . . .	6	1	1	4	3	8	10	0	0	7	3	10
Beatenberg . .	5	7	1	3	15	3	8	14	9	6	7	8
Caux . . .	5	9	10	3	17	0	8	16	5	6	9	4
Celerina . . .	6	13	2	4	11	9	10	19	11	7	16	7
Chamounix . .	6	3	7	4	4	4	9	16	5	7	1	6
Champéry . .	5	15	2	3	19	2	9	6	6	6	14	0
Château d'Oex .	5	15	2	3	19	8	9	5	4	6	14	0
Davos . . .	6	2	10	4	4	9	10	3	4	7	5	6
Engelberg . .	5	9	9	3	17	10	9	1	9	6	13	8
Grindelwald . .	5	11	3	3	18	3	9	2	6	6	13	7
Gstaad . . .	5	15	5	3	19	4	9	10	6	6	16	2
Lenk . . .	5	13	5	3	18	2	9	6	6	6	13	10
Les Avants . .	5	9	10	3	15	11	8	18	1	6	8	10
Les Ponts . .	5	2	8	3	10	11	8	13	11	6	5	3
Leysin . . .	5	11	10	3	18	7	8	19	10	6	12	0
Montana (including return Sierre-Montana) . . .	6	0	2	4	5	4	9	9	6	6	19	1
Mont Soleil . .	5	0	5	3	9	6	8	9	5	6	2	5
Mürren . .	5	13	2	4	0	2	9	5	6	6	16	7
Pontresina . .	6	13	8	4	11	9	10	19	11	7	16	7
Rigi Kulm . .	5	10	10	3	18	10	9	3	7	6	15	6
Saanen *via* Spiez and Zweisimmen .	5	15	11	3	19	9	9	11	6	6	17	0
Samaden . .	6	13	2	4	11	9	10	19	11	7	16	7
St. Moritz . .	6	13	2	4	11	9	10	19	11	7	16	7
Villars (including return Bex-Villars) .	5	14	4	4	0	11	9	0	8	6	12	8
Wengen . .	5	12	5	3	19	5	9	5	4	6	16	5
Zweisimmen . .	5	11	8	3	17	2	9	3	0	6	11	10

THE FOLLOWING CENTRES ARE REACHED BY SLEIGH

	1st Single	2nd Single	1st Return	2nd Return	Approximate length of sleigh due Time.
	£ s. d.	£ s. d.	£ s. d.	£ s. d.	
Adelboden. Frutigen for .	5 6 1	3 13 10	8 14 1	6 6 6	3 hours
Andermatt. Goschenen for	5 12 11	3 18 1	9 11 2	6 17 5	1 hour
Arosa. Chur for .	5 12 10	3 18 1	9 7 4	6 14 11	6½ hours
Ballaigues. Vallorbe for .	5 0 9	3 9 8	8 3 8	5 18 11	20 mins.
Campfer. St. Moritz for	6 13 2	4 11 9	10 19 11	7 16 7	20 mins.
Diablerets. Aigle for .	5 8 1	3 14 11	8 14 7	6 6 10	4½ hours
Grimmialp. Oey-Diemtigen for .	5 5 11	3 13 4	8 14 3	6 6 0	2½ hours
Kandersteg. Frutigen for .	5 6 1	3 13 10	8 14 1	6 6 6	2½ hours
Lenzerheide. Chur for .	5 12 10	3 18 1	9 7 4	6 14 11	3½ hours
Leukerbad. Leuk for .	5 14 7	3 19 6	9 4 9	6 13 10	4 hours
Morgins, Trois Torrents for	5 12 4	3 17 5	9 2 4	6 11 4	2 hours
Sepey. Aigle for .	5 8 1	3 14 11	8 14 7	6 6 10	3 hours

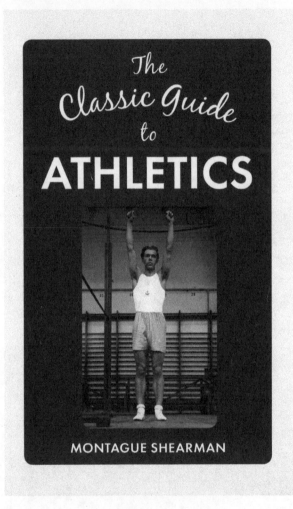

The
Classic Guide
to
ATHLETICS

MONTAGUE SHEARMAN

978-1-4456-4483-7

The
Classic Guide
to
FLY FISHING

H. CHOLMONDELEY-PENNELL

978-1-4456-4723-4

The *Classic Guide* to POLO

T. F. DALE

978-1-4456-4866-8